Martin Kragh (Ed.)

# Security and Human Rights in Eastern Europe
New Empirical and Conceptual Perspectives on Conflict Resolution and Accountability

With a foreword by Fredrik Löjdquist

Martin Kragh (Ed.)

# SECURITY AND HUMAN RIGHTS IN EASTERN EUROPE

New Empirical and Conceptual Perspectives on Conflict Resolution and Accountability

With a foreword by Fredrik Löjdquist

## Bibliografische Information der Deutschen Nationalbibliothek
Die Deutsche Nationalbibliothek verzeichnet diese Publikation in der Deutschen Nationalbibliografie; detaillierte bibliografische Daten sind im Internet über http://dnb.d-nb.de abrufbar.

## Bibliographic information published by the Deutsche Nationalbibliothek
Die Deutsche Nationalbibliothek lists this publication in the Deutsche Nationalbibliografie; detailed bibliographic data are available in the Internet at http://dnb.d-nb.de.

Cover graphic: ID 2901463 / Eastern Europe © Charon | Dreamstime.com

DOI: https://doi.org/10.24216/9783838216881_000

ISBN-13: 978-3-8382-1688-1
© *ibidem*-Verlag, Stuttgart 2022
Alle Rechte vorbehalten

Das Werk einschließlich aller seiner Teile ist urheberrechtlich geschützt. Jede Verwertung außerhalb der engen Grenzen des Urheberrechtsgesetzes ist ohne Zustimmung des Verlages unzulässig und strafbar. Dies gilt insbesondere für Vervielfältigungen, Übersetzungen, Mikroverfilmungen und elektronische Speicherformen sowie die Einspeicherung und Verarbeitung in elektronischen Systemen.

All rights reserved. No part of this publication may be reproduced, stored in or introduced into a retrieval system, or transmitted, in any form, or by any means (electronic, mechanical, photocopying, recording or otherwise) without the prior written permission of the publisher. Any person who does any unauthorized act in relation to this publication may be liable to criminal prosecution and civil claims for damages.

Printed in the EU

# Contents

Foreword by *Fredrik Löjdquist* ............................................................... 7

**Part I: Security and Human Rights in the Conflict Areas**

*Halya Coynash*
Human Rights Violations in the Occupied Parts of Ukraine's Donbas since 2014 ............................................................................. 11

*Stanislav Aseyev and Andreas Umland*
Prisoners as Political Commodities in the Occupied Areas of the Donbas in 2014-2021: The Use and Abuse of Detainees by the Russia-Supported Pseudo-States in Eastern Ukraine ...................... 29

*Victoria Roșa*
The Transnistrian Conflict 30 Years Looking for a Settlement ...... 43

*Diana Janse*
Georgia and the Russian Occupation ................................................ 73

*Stefan Meister*
Shifting Geopolitical Realities in the South Caucasus .................... 97

## Part II: Protracted Conflicts, European Security and International Law

*Stefan Wolff*
Conflict-Solving Mechanisms and Negotiation Formats for Post-Soviet Protracted Conflicts: A Comparative Perspective.... 127

*Andreas Umland*
Achievements and Limitations of the OSCE's Special Monitoring Mission in Ukraine's Donbas since 2014 ..................... 159

*John Zachau*
Russia's Instrumentalization of Conflict: The Protracted Conflicts as Open Wounds for European Security ....................... 181

*Marika Ericson and Isak Malm*
International Law and Accountability in Relation to the Protracted Conflicts in Eastern Europe .......................................... 193

# Foreword

DOI: https://doi.org/10.24216/9783838216881_001

A project on human rights and security in Eastern Europe was undertaken in 2021 related to the Swedish OSCE chairpersonship. This project was initiated by Dr. Martin Kragh and Dr. Andreas Umland at the then Russia and Eurasia Program at the Swedish Institute of International Affairs and was then taken over by the Stockholm Centre for Eastern European Studies when it was established in March 2021.

This was a major undertaking shedding light on how security, respect for democracy, human rights, rule of law and international law are interconnected in the conflicts in Eastern Europe. The relevance of these questions needs not be explained further as Russia continues and has escalated its aggression against Ukraine, in flagrant violation of international law and the principles and commitments underlying the European security order.

The project resulted in the texts gathered in this book, providing a rich source of analysis and policy recommendations on the conflicts in Eastern Europe.

Many important lessons are to be found in these texts: the interrelation between internal repression and external aggression, how the conflict managing mechanisms are in themselves part of the battlefield, how the framing and understanding of the nature of these conflicts play a crucial role, the effects of these conflicts on human security and human rights, etc.

Painful questions arise: have the efforts of the international community been conflict solving, conflict managing or conflict conserving? Has the ambiguity as to how to frame these conflicts—internal or interstate conflicts—been constructive or destructive? Have the attempts to "freeze" these conflicts contributed to lessen human suffering or prolonging and legitimizing violations of international law, including international humanitarian law?

It's my hope that the findings presented in this book continue to be studied by researchers, analysts, journalists, diplomats, politicians, military officers, civil society activists and practitioners of all kinds.

Given the very practical and political relevance of these questions, it's appropriate that this is the first book publication by the Stockholm Centre for Eastern European Studies. I sincerely thank the authors and everyone else who have contributed to this project, making this book possible.

*Fredrik Löjdquist*

Director of the Stockholm Centre for Eastern European Studies at the Swedish Institute of International Affairs

# Part I.

# Security and Human Rights in the Conflict Areas

# Human Rights Violations in the Occupied Parts of Ukraine's Donbas since 2014

*Halya Coynash*

DOI: https://doi.org/10.24216/9783838216881_002

## Executive Summary

*This report highlights human rights violations in the two self-proclaimed "republics" in the Donbas (Donets Basin) region of Ukraine since April 2014. Most such violations are the result of Russia's effective, yet persistently denied, political control over the pseudo-states. Former prisoners of the so-called Lugansk and Donetsk People's Republics have reported torture and the absence of fair trials, and also that a much larger number of captives are being held than officially acknowledged by the two satellite regimes. Ukrainian and independent media have been expelled from the occupied territories and replaced with outlets engaged in daily anti-Ukrainian propaganda and disinformation. Children and young people are being inculcated with a variant of Russia's military-patriotic education. Any future reintegration of the currently occupied parts of Ukraine's Donbas into the Ukrainian state will require more than the simple withdrawal of Kremlin interference. A number of policy recommendations are proposed to begin the reintegration process.*

## Introduction

There have been egregious abuses of political and civil rights in the occupied territories of eastern Ukraine since 2014. In *Freedom in the World 2020*, Freedom House gave what it refers to as Eastern Donbas (the Donets Basin) a score of 5 points out of 100 and a "Not Free" rating in its table of Global Freedom Scores. This was much lower than the score of 62 points and a 'Partly Free' ranking for the Ukrainian government-controlled areas and also considerably less than Russia's 20 points and even below occupied Crimea's 8 points.[1] Only Eritrea, North Korea, South Sudan, Syria, Tibet, Turkmenistan and Western Sahara were ranked below the separatist territories of the Donbas, in terms of political rights and civil liberties in 2020.[2]

The so-called Lugansk and Donetsk People's Republics (Russ. abbr.: LNR and DNR) are self-proclaimed republics, but have existed as de facto Kremlin-installed and guided puppet regimes since 2014. These fictitious statelets occupy roughly one-third of the whole of the Donbas in eastern Ukraine, as well as parts of Ukraine's Luhans'ka and Donets'ka *oblasts* — the Luhansk and Donets'k Regions. Although there are certain political differences between the two, similar human rights violations occur in both the LNR and the DNR.

This brief report highlights the major human rights issues in the occupied territories of the Donbas. The next section outlines a number of peculiarities of the two satellite regimes' political set-up and the consequences for human rights protection. Section 3 focuses on the severe limitations on mass media and political speech. Section 4 outlines the ongoing propaganda and militarization campaigns in the occupied territories of eastern Ukraine, especially those directed at young people. Section 5 deals with arbitrary imprisonment and systematic torture and section 6 illustrates the far-

---

[1] Freedom House, *Freedom in the World 2020: A Leaderless Struggle for Democracy*, December 2020. https://freedomhouse.org/sites/default/files/2020-02/FIW_2020_REPORT_BOOKLET_Final.pdf

[2] Freedom House, *Countries and Territories*, December 2020. https://freedomhouse.org/countries/freedom-world/scores

reaching restrictions on political and religious life. The concluding section formulates observations and policy recommendations for the Ukrainian state and Kyiv's various international partners, including the OSCE. This report provides only glimpses of the great range of human rights abuses in the two pseudo-states. Its recommendations cover only some of the most urgent — and by no means all of the necessary — measures required to improve the situation.

## Russia's Ambivalent Stance in the Donbas

Although the two pseudo-states are financed, armed and tightly controlled by Russia, Moscow has not formally recognized the LNR and the DNR. The Kremlin currently appears to view them as useful for undermining Ukrainian state- and nation-building. It also sees them as future instruments for influence on and destabilization of Ukraine as a whole. Moscow's official denial of its control over the LNR/DNR is one reason why the human rights situation there is even more dire there than in annexed Crimea. Being beyond the reach of Russian legislation and civil society, the territories of the LNR and the DNR lack even the low degree of transparency, the rudimentary rule of law and the partial public scrutiny of officials that exist in Russia.

For instance, as part of their "nationalization" drives, having gained control of parts of the Donbas, the LNR and the DNR have appropriated not only Ukrainian state enterprises, but also many companies belonging to people now living in government-controlled Ukraine. According to the eastern Ukraine NGO, Vostok SOS, such seizures have happened on a mass scale.[3]

---

3   Vostok SOS, *Report on rights violations in occupied Donbas in November 2020*, 7 December 2020. https://vostok-sos.org/vijskovi-zbori-v-l-dnr-ta-situacziya-z-covid-19-porushennya-prav-lyudini-na-tot-zafiksovani-u-listopadi/

Nevertheless, the territories of the LNR and the DNR are universally considered by Kyiv, Moscow and the West as still part of Ukraine. Against this background, international bodies have criticized the Ukrainian authorities for the ongoing situation that requires pensioners to travel to government-controlled areas of the Donbas to collect their Ukrainian pensions. However, there is no viable solution that would not in some way recognize the illegal republics or provide them with certain financial benefits from the Ukrainian state. The situation of pensioners in the occupied territories of the Donbas was already dire before 2020 but has become even more critical since the start of the COVID-19 pandemic. The resulting restrictions have made it very difficult for elderly people to travel to and from the government-controlled areas.

Putative judicial, law enforcement and governmental structures have been installed in the pseudo-states but, behind this facade, the two republics are little more than arbitrary fiefdoms ruled by Kremlin-installed local warlords. A variety of — often grave — human rights violations are commonplace. Especially brutal measures are meted out against Ukrainians who might reveal the involvement of Russian military and security service personnel in the LNR and the DNR. Halyna Haieva, for example, a 60-year-old nurse, was imprisoned and tortured in the notorious Izoliatsiia (Isolation) secret prison in Donetsk for compiling a list of Russian military service personnel treated in her hospital.[4]

In December 2020, the Chief Prosecutor of the International Criminal Court (ICC), Fatou Bensouda, announced that she had found reasonable grounds to believe that war crimes and other crimes against humanity that fall within the

---

4  B. Mashai, "'Izoliatsiia': place of pain and terror in Donetsk", 6 December 2019, https://zn.ua/ukr/personalities/izolyaciya-misce-bolyu-i-strahu-v-donecku-332154_.html

ICC's jurisdiction have been committed in both occupied eastern Ukraine and annexed Crimea.[5] Among those who provided testimony to the ICC were former victims of torture and incarceration in secret prisons such as Izoliatsiia and witnesses to extrajudicial executions.[6]

## Restrictions on Media Freedom

Every time that Russian and Russia-armed militants seized control of part of the Donbas in the spring/summer of 2014, they quickly blocked access to Ukrainian television. Within five days of the temporary capture of Slovians'k, for instance, the militants seized the television tower and replaced Ukrainian channels with Russian ones.[7] After occupying Donets'k, the largest city in the Donbas, in June 2014, the Russia-led separatists forced the removal of a number of Ukrainian television channels.[8] The militants justified their censorship by claiming that Ukrainian channels "incited enmity" and "discredited their republics".[9]

These actions had much to do with the enhanced role that Russian and pro-Russian local media outlets sought to play in the occupied zones in Crimea and the Donbas. In parallel with its military operation, Moscow conducted a

---

[5] *Statement of the Prosecutor, Fatou Bensouda, on the conclusion of the preliminary examination in the situation in Ukraine*, 11 December 2020, https://www.icc-cpi.int/Pages/item.aspx?name=201211-otp-statement-ukraine

[6] S. Aseyev and A. Umland, "'Isolation': Donetsk's Torture Prison", 4 December 2020.

[7] "Separatists in Sloviansk seize local television tower and cut Ukrainian television", 17 April 2014, https://novosti.dn.ua/news/205936-v-slavyanske-separatysty-zakhvatyly-mestnuyu-televyshku-y-vyklyuchyly-ukraynskoe-tv

[8] "In Donetsk, DNR forced providers to cut Ukrainian channels", 6 June 2014. https://news.liga.net/politics/news/v_donetske_dnr_zastavila_provaydera_otklyuchit_ukrainskie_kanaly

[9] "Press conference of the LNR ministry of information 'On the information security of the republic'", 12 November 2015, https://www.youtube.com/watch?v=P750ag_IL2U

deliberate campaign of defamation through its state-funded channels, which, among other things, spread the narrative that Ukraine's army was deliberately bombing civilians, that Kyiv was engaged in genocide.[10] One particularly revolting story reported that Ukrainian soldiers had "crucified" the young son of a separatist fighter.[11] In August 2015, some former employees of Russian state television channels admitted their involvement in this propaganda. One journalist reported that their editors-in-chief were instructed by the Kremlin to refer to Ukrainians as fascists and to the Kyiv government as a junta.[12]

In May 2020, a former manager of a television channel in occupied Horlivka gave himself up to Ukraine's Security Service (Ukr. abbr.: SBU) and provided insider information. According to his testimony, the media in the occupied territories is tightly controlled by the Russian Federal Security Service (Russ. abbr.: FSB) and the DNR's so-called Ministry of State Security (Russ. abbr.: MGB). The individual, who insisted on full anonymity, asserted that every channel has its own censor in the DNR MGB, who is told what can be shown and what is taboo.[13]

Access to the internet and social media is somewhat less restricted, although many websites, including the main Ukrainian sites providing information about Russian military engagement in the Donbas and countering disinformation, were already blocked within the first six months of

---

10  H. Coynash, "Russia Today's 'Genocide in eastern Ukraine': Sick, distorted and deleted", 16 July 2014. http://khpg.org/en/1405478412
11  H. Coynash, "New low in Russia's propaganda war", 14 July 2014, http://khpg.org/en/1405339370
12  D. Sidorov, "How they make TV-propaganda: Four testimonies", 6 August 2015, https://www.colta.ru/articles/society/8163-kak-delayut-tv-propagandu-chetyre-svidetelstva
13  TV Ukraina, "Testimony of a defector: exclusive interview about life under occupation", 24 May 2020. https://www.youtube.com/watch?v=nN3H40UoGLU&feature=emb_title.

the occupation. Over the years, official LNR policy, for example, has closely followed Russia's overt policy of officially blocking certain websites. By contrast, in 2019, the research agency DSLab Ukraine reported that it was unable to find a published list of officially banned websites in the DNR.[14]

There were still some independent Ukrainian and foreign journalists in the occupied parts of the Donbas in the first months of the conflict, but that soon changed. Several journalists were abducted and savagely tortured, and a few were held captive for several months. Since then, most people living in occupied Donbas have received information either mainly or solely from Russia- or LNR/DNR-controlled media outlets.

Stanislav Aseyev, a Donets'k blogger and journalist, spent 31 months in DNR captivity, including 28 months in the Izoliatsiia torture prison, because of some revealing reports he wrote under a pseudonym for the Ukrainian media.[15] Eduard Nedeliaev, a blogger from Luhans'k, received a 14-year prison sentence for "spreading negative information".[16] Ihor Halaziuk was held for two years for, among other charges, disclosing information about the Russian BUK anti-aircraft missile system, which had downed flight MH17, a Malaysian Boeing-777 airliner, over eastern Ukraine on July 17, 2014—and for using quotation marks around the words "Donetsk people's republic".[17]

---

14  "It has become known which sites are most often blocked by occupied Donbas providers", 6 August 2019, http Coyns://tech.informator.ua/2019/08/06/stalo-izvestno-kakie-sajty-chashhe-vsego-blokiruyut-internet-provajdery-ordlo/
15  S. Aseiev, "All occupied Donbas territory is one huge 'Izoliatsiia' concentration camp", 29 December 2020. https://www.pravda.com.ua/articles/2020/12/29/7278243/
16  H. Coynash, "Donbas militants 'sentence' blogger to 14 years for 'spreading negative information'", 2 August 2017. http://khpg.org/en/1501597083
17  H. Coynash, "Blogger spent 2 years in captivity for calling Russian-controlled Donbas occupied territory & writing the truth about MH17", 13 January 2020, http://khpg.org/en/1578702066

As of early 2021, there were several people serving 10-15-year sentences for "spying" based merely on pro-Ukrainian comments they made on social media. Maryna Yurchak, for example, was sentenced to 15 years in prison after being tortured in Izoliatsiia for media reposts and Twitter comments, such as calling the vehicles of top militants "orc-mobiles".[18] Yuri Shapovalov, a 55-year-old neuropathologist, was sentenced to 13 years for posts on Twitter which a DNR court alleged were "destabilizing the situation".[19] In his case, and in that of Pavlo Podvezko, who received a 14-year sentence for pro-Ukrainian comments on Twitter,[20] their video "confessions" to spying were almost certainly extracted through torture.

### Propaganda and Militarization

In contrast to the cases of Abkhazia and South Ossetia in Georgia, Russia has not recognized its proxy republics in Ukraine's Donbas and Moldova's Transnistria. Nonetheless, Moscow exerts similar psychological and ideological influence on the population of the two pseudo-republics. This includes the children in the DNR/LNR, who are exposed to a constant distortion of reality, and to anti-Ukrainian and pro-Russian propaganda. A May 2019 study by Kyiv's Institute for Mass Information found an alarming level of disinformation about Ukraine being spread in occupied Donbas, and

---

18  O. Omelianchuk, "15 years for a repost. The story of a Donetsk woman 'sentenced' in ORDLO", 22 April 2020. https://www.radiosvoboda.org/a/30568504.html

19  "Report and videoed 'confession' posted on the 'DNR ministry of state security' website", 15 May 2020. https://mgbdnr.ru/news.php?id=20200515_01&img_num=0

20  "Report and videoed 'confession' posted on the 'DNR ministry of state security' website", 11 February 2020, https://mgbdnr.ru/news.php?id=20200211_00&img_num=

that the amount of fake news had doubled in the previous two years.[21]

Both the DNR and the LNR have largely removed the Ukrainian language and most Ukrainian content from their school curriculums. School textbooks present an especially biased picture of the period since early 2014.[22] Children at both the preschool and school level are being taught that they should love and defend the Russian proxy republics, and that the Ukrainian state is their enemy. According to Vera Yastrebova, Head of the Eastern Human Rights Group, Russia is spending millions of dollars on projects aimed at developing pro-Kremlin views among young people in Ukraine's Donbas.[23]

In September 2019, for example, all school children in the DNR were taught the same "First Lesson": "The DNR is five years old: We are growing with the republic!" On the internet, instructions for these lessons called on children to become "true patriots of the DNR" and to "be prepared to defend their Fatherland". Lesson plans also contain summaries of "DNR history" for children to learn and that claim that a legitimate republic arose as the result of a spontaneous referendum on May 11, 2014.[24]

---

[21] "Fakes and hate speech: how Ukraine is presented in the media of occupied Donbas", *IMI*, 20 May 2019, https://imi.org.ua/articles/feyky-ta-mova-vor ozhnechi-iak-vysvitliuiut-ukrainu-v-media-okupovanykh-terytorly-donbasu-i47

[22] D. Durnev., "'Only five grades!' How the battle for schoolchildren of the self-proclaimed Donbas republics is playing out", 2 September 2019, https://spektr.press/tolko-pyat-ballov-kak-idet-borba-za-shkolnikov-samoprovozglashenny h-respublik-donbassa/

[23] "Occupied Mind. The threat that children's 'upbringing' in ORDLO holds for Ukraine", 21 January 2020, https://vchasnoua.com/articles/63702-okupovanyi-rozum-iaku-zahrozu-ukraini-nese-vykhovannia-ditei-v-ordlo

[24] "Plan for a single first lesson for Knowledge Day in the 2019-2020 school year on the topic 'DNR is five years old. We are growing with the republic!' for Grade 7", 2 September 2019, https://infourok.ru/let-dnr-rastem-vmeste-s-respublikoy-3821418.html

This is in line with the "program of patriotic education for children and young people of the DNR" adopted in 2017, which states that "patriotic education should become the main objective of the republic's state ideology as part of the Russian world ideology". The program also promotes systematic work to form "high patriotic consciousness, devotion to their Fatherland, readiness to carry out their civic duty and constitutional obligations in defending the interests of the DNR".[25]

To a great extent, the methods of indoctrination and militarization in the LNR and the DNR are identical to those in Crimea and Russia itself. Children take part in "military education" activities and are taught the "Russian world ideology". The most overtly militaristic of the various re-education programs for young people is the "Yunarmia" (Youth Army) project. Announcing the creation of this children's war training program in the DNR, Edward Basurin, deputy head of the People's Militia, asserted that "it is important to not only to bring youth up even more patriotically, but to fight against the falsification of history which the mendacious Kyiv authorities are currently involved in".[26] Young people swear allegiance to the unrecognized republics and are forced to commit to defend them against "enemies", most notably the Ukrainian state. Children from the occupied territories also take part in Russian competitions aimed at convincing them that they are part of a united Russian ethnicity.[27]

---

[25] "Program of patriotic education for children and young people of the DNR", 9 August 2017, http://mincult.govdnr.ru/sites/default/files/rasporiazhglavan252_09082017.pdf

[26] "A 'Young Guard—Yunarmia' movement will be created in DNR", 30 March 2019, http://gorlovka-news.su/novosti/novosti-gorlovki/12577-v-dnr-sozdadut-dvizhenie-molodaya-gvardiya-yunarmiya

[27] "Occupied Mind. The threat that children's 'upbringing' in DNR/LNR holds for Ukraine", 21 January 2020, https://vchasnoua.com/articles/63702-okupovanyi-rozum-iaku-zahrozu-ukraini-nese-vykhovannia-ditei-v-ordlo?fbclid=

In some regards, however, the official DNR and LNR mythology goes beyond the remembrance and education policies in Russia and Crimea. Thus, the "heroes defending the Fatherland" whom children are taught to glorify in the occupied Donbas territories include, among others, Arsen Pavlov, or "Motorola" (1983-2016), a Russian mercenary born in the Komi Republic.[28] Pavlov is believed to have killed several prisoners of war, including Ihor Branovyts'kyy, one of Ukraine's so-called Cyborgs, who had been defending the Donets'k Airport. Branovyts'kyy and other Ukrainian soldiers were taken prisoner in January 2015.[29]

Another officially celebrated martyr of the pseudo-republics is Aleksei Mozgovoi (1975-2015), an LNR military commander. In May 2014, Mozgovoi tricked the fighters he commanded into ambushing and killing a family heading to the Russian border for the money that they were carrying. Mozgovoi had told his fighters that the two cars were a convoy of dangerous Ukrainian ultra-nationalist Right Sector fighters. The parents were killed outright and their 10-year-old daughter was maimed for life.[30] In October 2014, Mozgovoi participated in the Novorossiia (New Russia) People's Court's first death sentence, passed by a show of hands.[31]

---

IwAR3QaAXIyVACfcSYyd_Q0lFn04W_zBfGJR4R83zYev-XnHZ6MlWPj8MJtt8

28  O. Sukhov, "'I killed 15 prisoners of war in Ukraine,' claims Russian fighter", 15 April 2015, www.theguardian.com/world/2015/apr/10/russian-fighter-ukraine-motorola
29  "How 'Motorola' killed a 'Cyborg' POW", 16 April 2015, https://www.bbc.com/ukrainian/politics/2015/04/150415_branovytsky_death_witness_sova_interview_vs
30  D. Kazansky, "How 'Novorossiya hero' Mozgovoy killed a whole family for money", April 2020, https://www.youtube.com/watch?v=ITm8XiNFLYI
31  *First Novorossiya people's court*. October 2014. https://www.youtube.com/watch?v=l8UQ76dSLuI

## Imprisonment and Torture in the Pseudo-Republics

As of January 2021, there were officially around 250 civilian prisoners in the LNR and the DNR, but there is no reliable way of estimating how many civilians have really been seized and are being held in various basements and secret prisons. Judging from the accounts of former captives, the number is significantly higher than the official figures given by the authorities in the pseudo-republics.

For instance, several miners who took part in an underground protest in June 2020 to demand pay arrears were imprisoned and probably tortured.[32] In many cases, however, there is no obvious political motive for arrests, and people either disappear or are sentenced to long terms of imprisonment in order to appropriate their property or businesses. For example, Roman Sahaidak was seized at Krasnodon in June 2017, shortly after refusing to sell his part of a company he jointly owned. His business partner is believed to have close contacts with people in the LNR MGB. Sahaidak was sentenced to 13 years in prison and the confiscation of his property, shortly after the release of his father, who had also been held hostage for several months.[33]

Both men and women have provided especially harrowing accounts of what they refer to as the "Izoliatsiia concentration camp" in Donets'k, including reports of torture involving electric currents being applied to fingers or genitals, and of teeth being extracted.[34] Former victims, such as the

---

32   D. Kazansky, "Arrests in Antratsyt. LNR militants have imprisoned striking miners", 10 June 2020. https://www.youtube.com/watch?v=yp1ww0mtpzU&feature=youtu.be&fbclid=IwAR2eSYUnPHQeVicLl1jRUjJmgLPiphUmMfwkyHCgMWy2jq_vYacQ9BtlFlo

33   H. Coynash, "Ukrainian gets 13-year 'sentence' for annoying friend of Russia-backed Luhansk militants", 3 December 2018, http://khpg.org/en/1543287388

34   J. Tschistjakowa, W. Schtscherbatschenko, S. Halling, *Menschenrechtsverletzungen in illegalen Gefängnissen und Haftanstalten in den nichtregierungskontrollierten Gebieten der Ostukraine.* 29 January 2021. www.laender-analysen.de/ukr

above-mentioned Halyna Haieva, have described how their torturers often inflicted pain "for their own entertainment" as much as to obtain information.

Stanislav Pechonkin spent almost three years in prison, most of that time in Izoliatsiia, after he was found with a photograph of the car of a local head of the DNR MGB, and to have made pro-Ukrainian comments on social media.[35] Detainees are often held at Izoliatsiia for up to a year and a half before being "tried" and sentenced to 10 to 15 years—frequently for "spying"—following a one-day hearing. Relatives who try to arrange independent lawyers to represent a prisoner are often unsuccessful. Attorneys are frightened to defend a person arrested by the LNR or DNR security services.

These and other violations of the right to a fair trial are outlined in a 2020 report by the UN Office of the High Commissioner for Human Rights (OHCHR), in which grave concerns over death sentences passed in the DNR were also raised.[36] There is nothing to suggest that such sentences were passed after a fair trial. Reporting the first of such confirmed sentences, the "acting head of the DNR military tribunal", Lyudmila Strateichuk, spoke of other cases where the death penalty was envisaged, saying that "these are cases of killings and of spying".[37] A large number of prisoners are given

---

aine-analysen/245/menschenrechtsverletzungen-in-illegalen-gefaengnissen-und-haftanstalten-in-den-nichtregierungskontrollierten-gebieten-der/

35 "'The paramedic could not resuscitate everybody:' Stanislav Pechonkin talks about 'Isolyatsia'", 4 February 2020, https://www.radiosvoboda.org/a/don bass-realii/30416486.html?fbclid=IwAR0GWN0CboWABfKcfwYo5LD_RGku 6kBRjOtiHGmTb9DIYCSq54ljPRyDoUs

36 "Human Rights in the Administration of Justice in Conflict-related Criminal Cases in Ukraine, April 2014—2020", OHCHR, https://ukraine.un.org/en/88 803-human-rights-administration-justice-conflict-related-criminal-cases-ukrai ne-april-2014-april

37 "Acting head of the military tribunal explains the article of the DNR criminal code on the exceptional measure of punishment", https://www.youtube.com/watch?v=NcbLiOkBypo

long sentences by the republics for supposed spying—a term often used for simple reporting or social media posting about the situation in occupied Donbas. The death sentences are over and above the extrajudicial executions known to have been carried out by militants in 2014 and the allegations of such killings reported by the OHCHR.[38]

Publicly professed support for the "Russian world" and the pseudo-republics is no guarantee of safety. Captives released from Izoliatsiia prison report that they were often held with former separatist fighters or others with pro-Russian views. At least two former DNR propaganda workers are now in prison. Oleksandr Bolotin, a member of the DNR civic chamber, has not been seen since his arrest on 21 January 2020.[39] Roman Manekin's third arrest in 2020 made him a record holder after his first two periods in "a basement" failed to prompt him to readjust his ideological affiliations. The Russian, who is well known for his strong anti-Ukrainian views, was arrested for a third time on 25 December 2020 on suspicion of "spying for Ukraine".[40]

### Restrictions on Political and Religious Life

While the LNR and the DNR each pretend to have two large competing political parties, in reality these scarcely differ. It is commonly understood that appointments to powerful posts are only made with the approval of Moscow. Any genuine opposition, including basically pro-Russian opposition,

---

38 "Report on the human rights situation in Ukraine 16 August to 15 November 2019", *OHCHR*, https://www.ohchr.org/EN/Countries/ENACARegion/Pages/UAReports.aspx
39 "What happened to pro-Russian blogger Bolotin in Donetsk?", 18 May 2020, https://www.radiosvoboda.org/a/30619197.html
40 "Blogger Roman Manekin detained in DNR in connection with possible collaboration with a Ukrainian security service agent", 28 December 2020. https://dan-news.info/pravoporyadok/zhurnalist-roman-manekin-zaderzhan-v-dnr-po-podozreniyu-v-shpionazhe-mgb.html

such as from the Communist Party, is not permitted in either republic. Even moderate criticism of people in high places can get the critic arrested, as seems to have been the case with the above-mentioned Oleksandr Bolotin.

While Russia has not officially recognized the DNR or the LNR, the Kremlin organized the arrival of politically biased, mostly far-right "international observers" to approve the illegal referendum conducted to legitimize the creation of the republics in May 2014, and then the first elections in November 2014. Moscow has also continued to push for local elections in the two republics before Ukraine regains control of its border with Russia, and without the demilitarization of the occupied territories. Such calls have received considerable support from some Western politicians and diplomats, even though free and fair elections cannot be effectively administered by heavily armed militants in conditions where a person can be imprisoned for a pro-Ukrainian tweet.[41]

The two Donbas pseudo-republics have also proved intolerant of Ukraine's rich religious diversity, and only recognize the Orthodox Church under the Moscow Patriarchate — even though it did not officially take a clear stand on the conflict in the Donbas. Human rights groups have presented detailed evidence of the persecution of other religious groups by the separatist militants in the Donbas, and of the role played by Russian irregulars in crimes against humanity in the occupied region.[42] A number of the paramilitary groups fighting Ukraine did so under the banner of Russian Orthodoxy, and some Moscow Patriarchate priests have been

---

41 "Local elections in DNR / LNR? What the advisers to the Normandy Four agreed on", 12 September 2020. https://www.bbc.com/ukrainian/news-54129456

42 "When God becomes the weapon. Report by the Centre for Civil Liberties and International Partnership for Human Rights", 6 May 2015. https://ccl.org.ua/wp-content/uploads/2013/07/When-God-Becomes-The-Weapon_6May2015_closed-for-editing.pdf

witnessed "blessing" militant fighters. When, in August 2014, Igor Druz confirmed to the BBC that his group had carried out extrajudicial killings in Slovians'k, purportedly "to prevent chaos", he did so as part of a self-described "Orthodox Christian" paramilitary unit.[43]

All faiths in the unrecognized republics, apart from the Orthodox Church under the Moscow Patriarchate, have been forced to "re-register". Such re-registration presents considerable ethical and legal challenges, especially for communities that are part of a greater, all-Ukrainian religious organization. This tactic is used as a weapon against those religious communities that decide to comply with the demand. Many re-registration applications were simply turned down, effectively outlawing the religious organizations. By October 2018, for example, most Protestant churches in the LNR had been refused re-registration.[44]

The last independent mosque in occupied Donetsk was closed in late June 2018, following an armed search and the interrogation of the mosque's imam and worshippers. Only those mosques that agree to be under the control of the militants have been able to function. In the occupied parts of the Donets'k *oblast*, these are under the strict surveillance of the DNR MGB.[45]

Both Donbas republics have imitated Russia in banning and energetically persecuting Jehovah's Witnesses. In the DNR, the Mormons are also banned, but this may primarily

---

43 "Strelkov's adviser confirms executions in Sloviansk", 2 August 2014. https://www.bbc.com/ukrainian/politics/2014/08/140802_separatist_executed_people_dk?ocid=socialflow_twitter

44 H. Coynash, "Russian controlled 'Luhansk republic' bans all Protestant churches", 17 October 2018, http://khpg.org/en/1539727352

45 "Donbas mosques which did not comply with the militants' demands were shut—Mufti Said Ismagilov", 19 November 2020, https://hromadske.radio/news/2020/11/19/na-donbasi-mecheti-iaki-buly-ne-zghodni-z-vymohamy-boyovykiv-zachyneni-muftiy-said-ismahilov

be linked to the appropriation Mormon real estate.[46] As a result of these and other similar actions, a considerable number of practicing believers of all faiths have fled the occupied territories.

## Implications for Ukrainian and Western Policies towards the Donbas

As indicated above, this report does not provide a full overview of the political situation or of human rights violations in the Donbas. The following observations are based on the author's long involvement in daily reporting on and analysis of the conflict.

1. Insofar as the human rights situation in occupied Donbas depends largely on Moscow, which has no incentive to end or even moderate the conflict in Donbas, harsher Western sanctions and other methods of exerting pressure need to be applied vis-à-vis the Kremlin.
2. It would be helpful if the OSCE, France and Germany, as participants in the Normandy Four negotiations, officially clarified their view on the exact sequence of developments that need to occur, according to the second Minsk Accords of February 2015, in order to reintegrate the occupied territories into the Ukrainian state.
3. As free and fair local elections in the currently occupied areas cannot take place until Ukraine regains full control of its border with Russia, and until Russian weapons have been withdrawn, no pressure should be exerted for Kyiv to agree to elections. An untenable situation, in which the OSCE Office for Democratic Institutions and Human Rights (ODIHR) observes an election that is one in name only, must be avoided.

---

46 D. Durnev, "If you want a quiet, untroubled life, pray for those in power", 23 November 2020, https://spektr.press/esli-hotite-imet-zhizn-tihuyu-i-bezmya tezhnuyu-molites-za-suschestvuyuschuyu-vlast-kak-liniya-fronta-v-ldnr-pode lila-pravoslavnyh-protestantov-musulman-i-drugie-konfessii/

4. Ukraine's government and its partners need to increase access to reliable information in the occupied Donbas, in both Russian and Ukrainian, about Ukraine and developments in the two pseudo-republics. The newly established specialist Ukrainian "Dim/Dom" (Home) television channel is a first step in this direction, but it provides insufficient information and does not reach deeply enough into the occupied territories. Among other things, new towers will need to be erected for transmission to the occupied territories.
5. Ukraine's government should ensure that young people from the occupied territories can easily enroll in educational institutions in the government-controlled parts of Ukraine, and that they are provided with adequate preparatory courses, for instance, to improve their Ukrainian language skills.
6. Detailed plans must be drawn up and published as a matter of urgency for the full reintegration of the occupied territories.
7. The propaganda that people in the occupied territories are exposed to, on the one hand, and the stereotypes that many Ukrainians have about people from occupied Donbas, on the other, must be countered more intelligently and systematically by the Ukrainian state and mass media.
8. Greater attention is required from all the relevant international bodies, including the OSCE, to ensure that Ukrainian civilian hostages and prisoners of war are not forgotten, and that increased pressure on Russia leads to an exchange of all captives.

*Halya Coynash is a member of the Kharkiv Human Rights Protection Group, which was founded in 1988. She is a prominent political analyst and a prolific columnist in Ukraine.*

# Prisoners as Political Commodities in the Occupied Areas of the Donbas in 2014-2021
The Use and Abuse of Detainees by the Russia-Supported Pseudo-States in Eastern Ukraine

*Stanislav Aseyev and Andreas Umland*

DOI: https://doi.org/10.24216/9783838216881_003

## Executive Summary

*Frozen or simmering post-Soviet territorial conflicts – such as the Russian-Ukrainian one in the Donets Basin (Donbas) in 2014-2021, but also those in South Ossetia, Abkhazia or Transnistria – have been destructive for several reasons. They typically involve multiple abrogation from international law, and from Europe's security order based on the Helsinki Final Act, the Paris Charter as well as other OSCE commitments. Often, they entail "gray zones" where neither international law nor the national legislation of a UN member state is enforced. The resulting lawlessness have had serious negative humanitarian implications, which often include grave human rights violations. This report highlights the fate of military and civilian detainees in the occupied Donbas and makes recommendations to address their widespread abuse. These prisoners and their exchanges have been significant issues in the Russian-Ukrainian conflict since 2014. They were also a recurring theme of the negotiations in Minsk. Thousands of combatants and civilians have been held captive. Their need for medical care, decent custody conditions and a speedy release continues to be a major topic of concern. In the past eight years, prisoner exchanges were transformed from an initially humanitarian into an increasingly political issue. More and more Donbas detainees were held by the Russia-led separatists, amid dubious accusations and frequent torture. They became de* facto hostages to be exchanged for political concessions, or for pro-Russia agents, irregulars and soldiers held by the Ukrainian state.

## Introduction

From April 2014 to February 2022, the Russian-Ukrainian armed conflict in Ukraine's Donets Basin (Donbas) claimed approximately 14,000 lives. In addition, tens of thousands of Ukrainians were maimed or traumatized, while several hundred thousand were displaced.[1] Less international attention was paid to the fate of the thousands of prisoners held and swapped by both sides in the conflict, or to the method of their exchange.[2]

In November 2015, it was reported that there were 79 places for the illegal detention of persons in the de facto Russia-occupied parts of the Donbas, or, as they were officially called, "Certain Districts of the Donets'k and Luhans'k regions (*Okremi rayony Donets'koy ta Luhans'koy oblastey* [ORDLO]).[3] According to the Security Service of Ukraine (the SBU), as of April 2019 the Ukrainian government had freed 3,233 Ukrainians from illegal detention.[4] Reliable data on the number and character of those altogether detained in the ORDLO are difficult to obtain as the self-proclaimed authorities were and are reluctant to disclose statistics.

---

1   The armed conflict in the Donbas is a "delegated interstate war" by Russia against Ukraine. See J. Hauter, "Delegated Interstate War: Introducing an Addition to Armed Conflict Typologies", *Journal of Strategic Security*, vol. 12, no. 4 (2019): 90–103, https://doi.org/10.5038/1944-0472.12.4.1756, https://schoolarcommons.usf.edu/jss/vol12/iss4/5/. For more on the nature of the war, see *Civil War? Interstate War? Hybrid War? Dimensions and Interpretations of the Donbas Conflict in 2014–2020*, edited by Jakob Hauter (Stuttgart: *ibidem*-Verlag, 2021).
2   T. Katrychenko, *Military and Civilian Detainees in Donbas: Searching for the Efficient Mechanism of Release* (Berlin: Deutsch-Russischer Austausch, 2019).
3   https://interfax.com.ua/news/general/307388.html.
4   https://jfp.org.ua/blog/blog/blog_articles/58?locale=en.

## The Dynamics of Prisoner Exchanges in 2014-2016

During the war's early hot period, in 2014-2015, it was relatively easy for Kyiv to retrieve its citizens from detention in the ORDLO. In the first year of the conflict, between April 2014 and April 2015, most of these prisoners of war (POWs) were combatants. Negotiations for their release often took place directly between field commanders on the spot, and not yet exclusively within the Minsk negotiations of the permanent Trilateral Contact Group (TCG) of Ukraine, Russia and the OSCE, and its various working subgroups. At the end of July 2014, according to official data from Ukraine's National Security and Defense Council (NRBO), 396 people, including three journalists, were held by the Russia-led separatists.[5]

One of the largest POW exchanges occurred shortly after the major Battle of Ilovays'k in the summer of 2014, which ended with the defeat of Ukrainian forces by Russian regular and irregular forces and the signing of a ceasefire protocol in Minsk on 5 September 2014. According to Ukraine's then President, Petro Poroshenko, approximately 1,200 service personnel were released from detention in the first four days after the agreement, and another 20 a few days later. However, 863 people remained captive.[6] By October 2014, Markiian Lubkivs'kyy, then an adviser to the head of the SBU, stated that close to 500 people remained prisoners in the self-proclaimed "Lugansk" and "Donetsk People's Republics" (LNR/DNR). Altogether, around 1,500 people had been freed since the start of the war.[7] On 26 December 2014, a large-scale exchange resulted in Ukraine's government handing over 222

---

5  https://lb.ua/news/2014/07/20/273481_plenu_terroristov_nahodyatsya_396.html.
6  https://interfax.com.ua/news/political/222349.html.
7  https://www.radiosvoboda.org/a/26635149.html#player-start-time=4.681382.

members of illegal armed groups, and receiving 150 soldiers of the Ukrainian armed forces in return.[8]

At the beginning of 2015, 110 Ukrainian soldiers were taken prisoner following the Battle of Debal'tseve. On 1 February 2015, a POW exchange led to Ukraine receiving 139 personnel while handing over 52 to the DNR/LNR.[9] In the first 18 months of the war, 2,957 Ukrainian citizens were freed.[10] Since the end of 2015, however, the number of people released through exchanges has declined sharply.

Four Ukrainian servicemen were released on February 20, 2016, and in early March 2016 the local journalist, Mariia Varfolomeeva, who had been accused of spying for the Ukrainian nationalist party "Right Sector", and who had been held captive for 419 days, was released by the LNR. In May 2016, the famous Ukrainian fighter and later politician Nadiia Savchenko was exchanged for two GRU officers following direct negotiations between Kyiv and Moscow.[11] Ukraine managed to free only 16 Ukrainian military and civilian prisoners in 2016.[12]

In 2016, the DNR/LNR began to actively use—mostly baseless—accusations of espionage and "extremism" to detain local civilians in the occupied territories (rather than those from the other side of the "contact line") in prisons and basements. More and more reports emerged of torture being used to force detainees to confess to being agents of the Ukrainian secret services. Civilian prisoners gradually replaced the previously captured and exchanged Ukrainian POWs. After 2015, POWs were no longer available in large

---

8   https://www.radiosvoboda.org/a/26764464.html.
9   https://www.pravda.com.ua/news/2015/02/20/7059227/.
10  https://jfp.org.ua/blog/blog/blog_articles/58?locale=en.
11  https://jfp.org.ua/blog/blog/blog_articles/58?locale=en.
12  https://www.radiosvoboda.org/a/news/28197607.html.

numbers for prisoner exchanges due to the reduced intensity of armed hostilities, at least until April 2021.

## New Developments in 2017-2021

In 2017, the issue of prisoner exchanges began increasingly to feature in general negotiations within the Minsk TCG and its various subgroups. The particulars of the exchanges became linked to other issues important to the DNR/LNR, such as their desire to be recognized as states. For instance, for some time, one of the most high-profile cases of political persecution in the ORDLO was that of the renowned historian and religious scholar, Ihor Kozlovs'kyy. Kozlovs'kyy was kidnapped from his hometown in Donets'k in January 2016 and held captive until December 2017, accused of keeping two grenades at his home. When his case drew internationally attention and the West began demanding his release, representatives of the Russian-led separatists insisted on calling Kozlovs'kyy a "DNR citizen". On this basis, the DNR quasi-authorities refused, prior to his eventual release, to include him in the ongoing prisoner exchanges.[13]

According to the SBU, as of August 2017, 137 people were being illegally held in the ORDLO. However, only 71 such cases were confirmed by representatives of the two pseudo-republics. Public announcements about the number of officially acknowledged prisoners have become a method for the local quasi-authorities to exert political pressure on Kyiv. Even though the Ukrainian government presented hard evidence of more detainees than those acknowledged by the DNR/LNR, the latter refused to confirm that these people were in custody. It was only when Ukraine made

---

13 https://lb.ua/society/2017/02/16/358871_dnr_otkazivaetsya_vidat_ukraine.html.

concessions in the political subgroup at the Minsk TCG negotiations, and allowed the Ukrainian politician Viktor Medvedchuk, whose daughter's godfather is Vladimir Putin and who is close to the Russian President, to present the next prisoner exchange as his own personal success, that additional prisoners were acknowledged.[14] Also in 2017, the DNR/LNR began to demand the release of Kyiv-held prisoners who had a criminal history and little to do with the military conflict in the Donbas.[15]

A large prisoner exchange took place at the end of 2017. Ukraine handed over 233 people and the DNR/LNR in return released 73 detainees. Ihor Kozlovs'kyy, who by then had been detained for almost two years, was freed along with 59 Ukrainian military personnel and civilians. The latter had been accused of espionage or extremism, and were used for political purposes during the negotiations in the humanitarian subgroup of the Minsk TCG.[16]

Throughout 2018, the number of civilians detained in the DNR/LNR increased. They were sometimes arbitrarily arrested in the streets of occupied Donbas. Often, those arrested were thrown into basements, put under pressure or tortured, and forced to confess to having been engaged in espionage, terrorism or extremism on behalf of Ukraine, i.e. the so-called "exchange articles". In this way, the DNR/LNR built up a peculiar "exchange fund" of prisoners to be used as political commodities in negotiations with Kyiv.

On 28 June 2019, Viktor Medvedchuk mediated the recovery of four Ukrainian prisoners who were unilaterally released from the ORDLO. This highly publicized act by the

---

14   https://gordonua.com/news/war/medvedchuk-obmen-27-dekabrya-2017-goda-sostoyalsya-isklyuchitelno-blagodarya-putinu-231845.html.
15   https://www.bbc.com/ukrainian/features-40774670
16   https://hromadske.ua/posts/velykyi-obmin-koho-zvilnyly-z-polonu-boiovykiv-na-donbasi

manifestly pro-Kremlin Medvedchuk marked another step in the transformation of the DNR/LNR discharge of prisoners into an instrument of political propaganda. This was the first release Moscow had agreed to in a period of 18 months. The four were initially handed over not to officials in Kyiv, but to a Ukrainian political actor well-known for his ties to the Kremlin.[17]

A large prisoner exchange took place on 29 December 2019. The Ukrainian government gave up 124 detainees and received 76 from the DNR and the LNR, 64 of whom were civilians and only 12 constituted military personnel. Some of the POWs had been held for several years. This indicates that the continuously operating detention facilities in the ORDLO had become more and more full of civilians, often imprisoned for "incorrect behavior" on social networks.

In a smaller prisoner exchange on 16 April 2020, the Ukrainian government received 20 people and handed over 14 to the DNR/LNR. A number of the detainees transferred from the ORDLO to Ukrainian government-controlled territory in this exchange had criminal records. Paradoxically, some had even been temporary members of illegal pro-Russian "insurgent" armed groups. For example, Oleksandr Sadovs'kyy, who had been exchanged in mid-April 2020, was arrested by the Ukrainian police two weeks later on a charge of large-scale organized fraud.[18] Another man delivered to the Ukrainian government, Volodymyr Karas, was accused of working for the DNR police.[19]

---

17  Katrychenko, *Military and Civilian Detainees in Donbas*, 18.
18  https://www.unian.ua/society/obmin-polonenimi-na-donbasi-oleksandr-sa dovskiy-zaareshtovaniy-sudom-kiyeva-pishut-grati-novini-ukrajini-10986920. html.
19  https://www.pravda.com.ua/rus/articles/2020/04/16/7248193/.

## The Treatment and Purpose of Detainees in the DNR/LNR

The illegal detention and torture of prisoners in the ORDLO has become more widely discussed in the Ukrainian and international media since 2018, attention focusing in particular on one of the DNR's most brutal places of incarceration, the secret so-called *Izoliatsiia* (Isolation) prison on the *Svitly shliakh* (Light Path) Street in Donets'k. One of the authors of this report, Stanislav Aseyev, who had clandestinely worked as a reporter in the ORDLO for Radio Liberty, was held there throughout 2018. The DNR did not allow representatives of the OSCE or the International Committee of the Red Cross (ICRC) to meet Aseyev after he had been arrested in May 2017.

Among other *Izoliatsiia* prisoners who gained prominence as a result of their detention were a young Jordanian physician, arrested at a checkpoint in the ORDLO, and a neuropathologist detained on the streets of Donets'k by the DNR's so-called Ministry of State Security (MGB), who was given a 13-year prison sentence.[20] A video of his kidnapping by the MGB contains his confession to espionage and a call to fellow citizens not to cooperate with the Ukrainian government—a statement probably given under duress.

From Aseyev's first-hand observations during his 28-month term in *Izoliatsiia*, more than 100 civilians were processed and tortured there in 2018-2019. Most were accused under the above-mentioned exchange articles of extremism, terrorism and espionage, which made them eligible for prisoner exchange with the Ukrainian government. In their conversations with Aseyev, most reported physical and

---

20 http://khpg.org/en/1589828711.

psychological torture, which could include mock executions or rape. Some were forced to do hard physical labour.

The maltreatment in *Izoliatsiia* has been extensively documented by, among others, the United Nations Office of the High Commissioner for Human Rights (OHCHR) in a 2020 report.[21] Based on numerous witness testimonies, the official UN survey details various forms of "beatings during interrogations", and other forms of abuse. "For example, one detainee was tied to the table, handcuffed and hooded. Perpetrators attached one electrode to his genitalia and inserted a metal tube with a second electrode into his anus. [...] Some detainees held in 'Izoliatsiia' could not prevent themselves from urinating and defecating during electrocution". Sexual abuse is also frequent in *Izoliatsiia*. According to the UN report: "One detainee told OHCHR that while in 'Izoliatsiia', he heard guards scream at female detainees on their way to the shower: 'Go shave your [vaginas]. You are about to go upstairs to work it off.'"

Several detainees reported that a health professional was present during their interrogations: "The man revived those who lost consciousness, and guided the perpetrators about how to torture to inflict maximum pain without causing death. He also examined detainees before the torture and asked about their medical conditions; measured their blood pressure or pulse; and gave injections".[22] These practices are not limited to the *Izoliatsiia* prison, nor have they been documented by the OHCHR alone. A variety of governmental and non-governmental Ukrainian and non-Ukrainian

---

21  United Nations, Office of the High Commissioner for Human Rights. *Report on the Human Rights Situation in Ukraine, 16 November 2019 to 15 February 2020* (Kyiv: OHCHR, 2020), 38-42.
22  Ibid.

organizations have collected similar testimonies related to various locations in occupied Donbas.[23]

The DNR's and LNR's harsh treatment of prisoners is not just an expression of sadism. It serves a rational political function for the pseudo-states. The frequent threat and use of torture within the ORDLO, in addition to deterring opposition to the DNR/LNR leadership, is used to extract preformulated "confessions". Prisoners are then eligible to be swapped with soldiers and allies held by the Ukrainian authorities. The OHCHR concludes that the ill-treatment "usually continued until a detainee agreed to confess (orally, in writing or on video) or to provide information".[24] Aseyev also observed frequent occurrences of sadistically motivated torture during his time in detention.

Oddly, in addition to pro-Ukrainians and accidental civilians, numerous former "rebels" (*opolchentsy*) or former DNR/LNR volunteer fighters or mercenaries from both Ukraine and Russia were held in *Izoliatsiia* and other detention facilities. Whether Russian citizens or not, many of them are also prosecuted under articles making reference to "high treason" or "illegal possession of weapons". Apparently, most convictions of these detainees are also based on confessions extracted through torture. During his more than two years at *Izoliatsiia*, Aseyev personally met and talked to ten pro-Russian and Russian soldiers and civilians, including a Colonel, a Major General, two Lieutenant Colonels, a Captain, a Senior Lieutenant and a Major who had all previously served in various DNR units, as well as a Lieutenant in the Russian Navy. There were also other pro-Russian Ukrainian or Russian citizens. They were treated as harshly as

---

23 See the various reports and numerous articles published by, among others, the Kharkiv Human Rights Protection Group, the "Justice for Peace in Donbas" Coalition, Human Rights Watch and the European Parliament.

24 *Office of the United Nations High Commissioner for Human Rights Report*, 14.

supposedly pro-Ukrainian detainees and often also sentenced to long prison terms.

From the middle of 2020 onwards, representatives of the DNR/LNR refused to submit further lists of those they would like to swap with Kyiv at the Minsk talks, even though the Ukrainian government provided lists of desired returnees to the OSCE.[25] One of the political conditions for an exchange stipulated by DNR/LNR emissaries was that the Ukrainian Parliament reformulate a resolution it had adopted earlier in 2020. This Rada declaration touches on future local elections in the ORDLO and has been categorically condemned by Russia.[26] Despite reminders by the OSCE Coordinator of the TCG Humanitarian Working Subgroup, Toni Frisch, that political demands should not obstruct resolution of humanitarian issues, DNR/LNR representatives halted the exchange of prisoners, insisting that the text of the Rada resolution be changed.

The relevance of this issue declined following Ukraine's October 2020 local and regional elections. Instead, at the end of 2020, representatives of the DNR/LNR set new preconditions for further prisoner exchanges. They demanded the deletion of the criminal records of nine former Ukrainian detainees, and Kyiv's acceptance of a so-called peace plan for the Donbas proposed by the DNR/LNR.[27] As a result of these new positions at the Minsk negotiations, the continuation of the earlier prisoner exchange practice was again stalled, as Russia and its marionette regimes in the ORDLO transformed their detainees into political commodities.

---

25  https://www.ukrinform.ua/rubric-ato/3117560-ukraina-peredala-do-tkg-spiski-polonenih-bojoviki-poki-movcat.html.
26  https://suspilne.media/57330-kravcuk-poprosiv-zminiti-postanovu-pro-miscevi-vibori-na-vimogu-ordlo-i-rosii/.
27  https://lb.ua/society/2020/12/18/473356_rosiya_blokuie_obmin_polonenimi_i.html.

## Policy Recommendations

In 2021, there was a deadlock in the prisoner exchange process as the often horrific situation and frequent torture of detainees in the basements and prisons of the DNR/LNR, such as *Izoliatsiia*, continued. A number of steps would have helped to improve the human rights situation more generally, and eased the fate of detainees in the two pseudo-republics in particular:

1. *Monitoring and documentation*: Mechanisms should be explored and developed for observing illegal detentions more closely and recording the fate of detainees more systematically in the DNR and LNR, and other occupied territories. In 2014-2021, the OSCE Special Monitoring Mission should have expanded its focus to include additional social patrolling in its work program and more results from investigating non-military affairs, including human rights violations, in its reports. The ICRC, United Nations and other governmental entities and NGOs should cooperate with each other and with local media outlets, administrations and NGOs on joint production of a comprehensive register of incarcerations and captives, and of detailed descriptions of individual cases. Additional organizations such as the International Humanitarian Fact-Finding Commission,[28] and other specialist human rights groups and investigative agencies not yet present in Ukraine, should be encouraged to become active in the country and to apply their expertise to, among other things, researching the situation of prisoners. The Commissioner for Human Rights of the Council of Europe should include the human rights situation in DNR/LNR and other occupied regions in her reporting on Ukraine, without legitimizing the de facto authorities. The detailed reports of the OHCHR provide a good model.
2. *Alleviation and release*: Western governments should insist on full access for the ICRC and other humanitarian

---

28  https://www.ihffc.org/index.asp.

organizations to all those imprisoned. International governmental organizations and legal mechanisms, such as those of the United Nations or the Council of Europe, should be mobilized to ease the fate of prisoners in the DNR/LNR torture jails. The transfer of detainees to Ukraine's government-controlled area or their release as well as the prevention of new unlawful detentions of civilians should be high priorities in the West's negotiations with Moscow. The OSCE Chairpersonship and its participating states should exert maximum pressure on Moscow to end the DNR's and LNR's widespread use of physical and psychological torture in their various jails. The OSCE and Normandy Format partners should have insisted on reviving the practice of regular prisoner exchanges in the Donbas. The pro-Russian side's proposed idea of making the release of additional DNR/LNR prisoners conditional on meeting the two pseudo-republics' political demands should be comprehensively rejected. The resolution of basic humanitarian issues (in addition to fundamental security issues) should instead become a precondition for negotiations on the political demands of Russia and its satellite regimes. A public modification of the official position of the European Union could emphasize that observing basic civil and human rights in the ORDLO and other occupied territories is—along with resolving other fundamental issues, such as re-establishing the Ukrainian government's full control over the Russian-Ukrainian border—a necessary first step towards starting a political process in the currently occupied territories.

3. *Accountability and prosecution*: The specialist human rights protection organs and international courts should become more involved in the investigation of human rights abuses in Ukraine's occupied territories. Competent institutions such as the Council of Europe Human Rights Commissioner and the OHCHR are already present in the region, and should become even more active in bringing the dire situation of political detainees in mainland Ukraine and Crimea to the attention of governments and the public

worldwide.[29] Relevant international legal institutions, such as the European Court on Human Rights and International Criminal Court, should be actively used to probe human rights violations and punish criminal behavior in the occupied parts of Ukraine. A separately designated EU and US sanctions regime could be designed and implemented in connection with the abuses by officials in the Donbas pseudo-republics and the Russian occupation regime in general, and with the horrific practices of detention and torture, in particular.

4. *For further consideration*: The gross violations of fundamental rights raised in this report pose more general questions about the applicability of international law as well as the relevance of European human rights commitments, such as those made within the OSCE and the Council of Europe, in these and similar cases. This concerns, in particular, the implementation of international humanitarian law in the conflict zones of the protracted conflicts in Eastern Europe, and the possibility of eventually holding the perpetrators of crimes such as those indicated above to account. These complicated issues merit greater international analytical and political attention, both within the framework of practical efforts to manage and resolve these conflicts and in relevant academic and legal discussions on these topics.

*Stanislav Aseyev works as an Expert on the occupied parts of the Donbas at the Ukrainian Institute for the Future (UIM) in Kyiv, and is author of the book "The Light Path: History of a Concentration Camp" (L'viv, 2020). Andreas Umland is an Analyst at the Stockholm Centre for Eastern European Studies of the Swedish Institute of International Affairs (UI). The present report was completed in spring 2021, and reflects the situation up until at that time.*

---

29  https://www.ohchr.org/en/countries/enacaregion/pages/uaindex.aspx.

# The Transnistrian Conflict
## 30 Years Looking for a Settlement

*Victoria Roşa*

DOI: https://doi.org/10.24216/9783838216881_004

## Executive Summary

*For international diplomacy, European geopolitics and the academic study of protracted conflicts, the 30-year-long confrontation between the post-Soviet Moldovan government and a separatist pseudo-state supported by Moscow has become a familiar, if not archetypical, case. This report outlines the genesis of the Transnistrian conflict focusing on its public perception in and outside Moldova as well as on the settlement process that has brought no substantial results so far. The lack of a solution to the Transnistria issue poses larger questions about the usefulness of existing conflict resolution formats and processes. These approaches to solving the conflict create the misleading impression that the issue is purely internal to Moldova, with Russia playing the role of an impartial mediator and provider of peacekeeping forces. They also focus on local confidence-building measures rather than on larger geopolitical challenges, such as the unwanted Russian military presence on the territory of the Republic of Moldova. The Moldovan experience indicates that a sustainable solution to such conflicts, based on respect for international law as well as OSCE principles and commitments, is impossible without more emphasis on the accountability of Moscow. Applying instruments for domestic and civil conflict resolution to what are interstate conflicts is misleading and risks not only prolonging such confrontations but even making them more difficult to solve.*

*Once regarded as the secessionist dispute easiest to end in the post-Soviet region, the Transnistrian conflict continues to remain unresolved. Following the collapse of the Soviet Union, the conflict was determined by political-economic and military rather than ethnic or religious factors.*[1] *Large-scale armed violence including a Russian military intervention in 1992 left the newly independent Republic of Moldova with deep wounds, the inability to constitutionally control its full territory being only one.*

## Some Basic Facts

The Transnistrian region is a breakaway region incorporating 12 percent of Moldova's territory, mainly on the eastern shores or "left bank" of the Nistru River. It comprises 10 percent of Moldova's population or approximately 350,000 people, made up of three roughly equal groups of ethnic Moldovans, Russians and Ukrainians.[2] All of these groups are mainly Russian-language speakers. Thus, the region was and is subject and accessible to Moscow's foreign policy ambitions and so-called compatriots' policies. At present, the officially accepted terms for the two conflicting parties are the Republic of Moldova, represented by its constitutional authorities ("right bank"), on the one side, and the Transnistrian region, represented by its local leaders ("left bank"), on the other. Following meetings of the Helsinki Committee of Senior Officials (CSO) and Commonwealth of Independent States (CIS), an Agreement between Moldova and Russia on the principles of a peaceful settlement of the armed conflict in Transnistria was signed in Moscow, on July 21st, 1992. The document comprises eight chapters on, among other subjects, an immediate end to armed hostilities and a future conflict settlement.[3] The 1992 ceasefire agreement was justified, at the

---

1 A. Gvidiani, *Culegere de articolepe problematica transnistreană (2016-2020)* (Chișinău: n., 2020), 128.
2 Ibid.
3 "Soglashenie o printsipakh mirnogo uregulirovaniia vooruzhennogo konflikta v Pridnevstrovskom regione Respubliki Moldova". *Pravitel'stvo Respubliki*

time, as it ended the bloodshed. Over the years, however, it has met with increasing criticism, mostly due to its not being fulfilled in good faith. The most important issues addressed in the document are:

1. A complete ceasefire and the establishment of a demilitarized Security Zone;
2. The setting up of a tripartite Joint Control Commission (JCC) with the mandate to coordinate the operational activity of a peacekeeping mission under a so-called Trilateral Joint Military Command. The peacekeeping mission consisted initially of five Russian, three Moldovan and two Transnistrian battalions. According to the so-called Odessa Agreement of 1998, the number of peacekeepers was decreased to 500 soldiers from each of the three sides;[4]
3. Prevention of sanctions and blockades, as well as of any impediments that could restrict the movement of people, goods and services;
4. Commitment of the Russian Army contingents stationed on the territory of Moldova to observe neutrality while questions regarding their status and withdrawal should be discussed between Moldova and Russia.

Central issues, such as the Russian military contingent's stationing in Moldova, hindrances to the movement of people, goods and services, and violations of the Security Zone, and the legal status of the Transnistrian region are still matters of ongoing negotiation.

## Conflict Resolution Impediments

The Transnistrian region's disputed status, as well as Russia's ambiguous role in the settlement process and its general

---

*Moldova*, 21 July 1992, https://gov.md/sites/default/files/1992-07-21-ru-moscow-agr_on_principles_of_peaceful_settlem.pdf.

4 "Agreement on Confidence Measures and Development of Contacts between Republic of Moldova and Transdniestria", *OSCE*, 20 March 1998, https://www.osce.org/files/f/documents/6/d/42310.pdf.

geopolitical interests in Eastern Europe have conditioned the conflict solution attempts and regional security agenda. In the last 30 years, both Chișinău's approach to domestic reintegration and conflict resolution efforts by foreign actors have shaped the evolution of the negotiations and the current status quo. The Russian Federation's assertive foreign policy towards Moldova, its assistance to the separatists, and its periodic embargoes of Moldovan goods have drawn only vacillating attention, by the EU and US, to the settlement negotiation process and confidence building projects.

Moldova's zigzagging domestic political context has also hindered the formulation of a widely agreed national reintegration policy. The conflict in Georgia in August 2008, the annexation of Crimea in March 2014 and the continuous fighting in Ukraine's Donbas have brought the Transnistrian conflict into a new light. In particular, the Russian military contingent that continues to be stationed in the Transnistrian region without consent from the government in Chișinău has acquired a new symptomatic quality.

In the early 1990s, the seeming ease of a settlement of the conflict rested on the widespread assumption that it was a secessionist struggle with domestic political roots. Today, the nature of the conflict nature has become a more disputed matter, generating heated discussions within Moldova. The conflict is referred to either as a civil and elite conflict, or as an interstate confrontation initiated by Moscow's aggression, and even as an entirely artificial issue resulting from the malign influence of the Russian Federation.

Moldova's internal debate about how to interpret the conflict touches upon two factors whose effects could pave the way to conflict settlement. First, the debate has raised the issue of an effective reintegration policy that considers the costs of reunification, both financial and political. The current debate has brought forward the need to formulate a nationwide reconciliation strategy that would counteract the disinformation and false narratives feeding the conflict.

In the Moldovan public debate, the Transnistrian conflict is today often described as driven by disinformation promoted by the secessionist movement's leaders.[5] Their narratives, in particular, refer to the alleged suppression of the Russian language, the threat of Moldova unifying with Romania, and Chişinău's pro-Western orientation as the main reasons for Transnistria's call for self-determination in 1992. The allegedly imminent imposition of the Romanian language and annexation of Moldova by Romania are key themes of secessionist discourse.

On August 31, 1989, the Romanian language, with its Latin alphabet, was given the status of Moldova's official language. This change was embraced by the Moldovan-majority population as a symbol of national recovery and independence. Being an act of national emancipation, it was criticized, however, by large sections of the Russian-speaking minorities, mainly by ethnic Russians and Ukrainians, even though Russian remained the language of interethnic communication.

For 30 years, Chişinău's allegedly misconceived Western orientation has been constantly used by separatist and pro-Russian forces to generate division between the banks of the Nistru River. Media in the Transnistrian region depicts the Republic of Moldova as an aggressor and a "neighboring country" planning to unite with Romania and join NATO, renounce Christian and Orthodox family values, as well as

---

5  "Transdniestrian Conflict: Origins and Main Issues", *OSCE*, n. d., https://www.osce.org/files/f/documents/4/3/42308.pdf.

exterminate Russian-language speakers.[6] Nevertheless, today the most important export market for the economy of the separatist pro-Russian Transnistrian region is the West. According to data provided by the region's so-called customs authority, in the first half of 2021, the EU's share in the Transnistrian region's exports was 37.8 percent of total exports (US$150.6 million) compared to the 9 percent share of the Russian Federation (US$35.5 million). Romania and Poland account for 70 percent of the EU's share of the Transnistrian region's exports, amounting to US$47.13 million for Romania and US$59 million for Poland.[7]

Transnistria's international competitiveness is largely based on enormous Russian gas subsidies. The separatists are not paying market value for their imported Siberian natural gas and have now accumulated a debt to Gazprom that amounts to approximately US$7.5 billion. The debt is officially due to be paid by the Republic of Moldova but remains unrecognized by the Moldovan constitutional authorities, who have no control over Transnistria's gas imports from Russia.[8] With this scheme in place since the 1990s, the Russian Federation keeps Moldova as its hostage and heavily subsidizes the Transnistrian region.

In 2021, 95 percent of the Transnistrian region's exports to Romania and Poland represented metal and metal products from the Rîbnița metallurgical factory known by the acronym MMZ. This industrial enterprise benefits from heavily

---

[6] V. Rosa, "Disinformation Muddles Transnistrian Conflict Resolution", *Institute for War and Peace Reporting*, 26 August 2020, https://iwpr.net/global-voices/disinformation-muddles-transnistrian-conflict-resolution.

[7] "Rusia salvatoare? Economia transnistreană supraviețuiește datorită UE și Moldovei", *Mold Street*, 22 July 2021, https://www.mold-street.com/?go=news&n=12391.

[8] S. Tofilat and V. Parlicov, "Russian Gas and the Financing of Separatism in Moldova", *Free Russia*, 14 August 2020, https://www.4freerussia.org/russian-gas-and-the-financing-of-separatism-in-moldova/.

subsidized gas prices and is under the control of Russian capital. The Russian gas subsidy stimulates political corruption on both banks of the Nistru River, finances separatism, as well as, indirectly, contributing to the entire region's insecurity.

The local authorities of the Transnistrian region and the autonomous territorial unit of Gagauzia in southern Moldova favor the continuation of Soviet traditions and orientation towards Russia. In the two regions, "referenda" were conducted asking the local populations about their foreign policy preferences. On September 17, 2006, the Transnistrian region residents were asked to choose between joining Moldova or becoming independent and a part of the Russian Federation. According to official data provided by the local separatist authorities, 97.2 percent of the residents allegedly voted for independence and unification with the Russian Federation. These results were, however, not recognized by Moldova's constitutional authorities.[9] The referendum was a result of the Transnistrian leaders' disagreement with new customs regulations introduced by Chișinău aimed at reducing corruption and smuggling, and of resentment concerning travel restrictions regarding the Schengen area imposed by the EU on the separatist leaders, who had repeatedly sabotaged the negotiation process.

## From Violent to Protracted Conflict

Before the conclusion of the above-mentioned ceasefire agreement in summer 1992, the Transnistrian secessionists had been backed by irregular Cossack units from Russia, by the 14th former Soviet and then Russian Army, as well as by

---

9   D. Minzarari, "The Gagauz Referendum in Moldova: A Russian Political Weapon?", *Eurasia Daily Monitor*, 5 February 2014, https://jamestown.org/program/the-gagauz-referendum-in-moldova-a-russian-political-weapon/.

volunteer fighters from other parts of the Soviet Union. This escalated existing domestic tensions into full-scale war.[10] The 1992 fighting resulted in 1,132 deaths on both sides, among them 310 civilians. More than 3,500 persons were wounded. Approximately 130,000 people were internally displaced while approximately 70,000 migrants from the war region sought refuge in Russia, Ukraine, and Belarus.[11] Chișinău lost control over the Transnistrian region's territory.

Since the ceasefire, no large-scale violence has occurred, the conflict becoming protracted.

The now almost 30-year-long negotiation process has brought few results. The mediation agenda includes "three baskets": (a) socio-economic issues; (b) legal, humanitarian, and human rights issues; and (c) political and security issues. The third basket envisages a comprehensive settlement of the conflict including a definition of the future political status of the Transnistrian region within the Republic of Moldova, and the withdrawal of Russian troops and ammunition from its territory. Yet little has been achieved so far.

Today, the negotiations between Chișinău and Tiraspol are organized within two frameworks. There is a 1+1 format between Moldova's government and the secession's leaders. This format also includes 11 thematic working groups and three subgroups. Until 2002, there was also a 3+2 format that included the OSCE, Russia and Ukraine as mediators. As a result of the 2005 so-called Odessa Protocol, this format was

---

10  "Case of Ilascu & Others v. Moldova & Russia (Application no. 48787/99)", *European Court of Human Rights*, Strasbourg, 8 July 2004, http://www.rulac.org/assets/downloads/Ilascu_v_Moldova_and_Russia.pdf.
11  E. Gorelova and G. Selari, "The costs of the Transnistrian conflict and the benefits of its resolution", Chișinău, 2009, http://www.cisr-md.org/pdf/Report%20ROM%20Master%20Draft%20vEG.pdf.

upgraded to the current 5+2 format, with the US and the EU as observers.[12]

The negotiations follow a tactic of small steps, which implies the resolution of mainly socio-economic problems, and confidence-building measures. This approach was chosen to prepare the ground for a later comprehensive settlement of the conflict that would include an end of the Russian military presence. Even though it has brought little movement in this direction, the small-steps tactic was reinforced as a result of negotiations in Berlin in 2016, after a two-years break in official contacts between the conflicting sides. To prepare a solution concerning political and security issues, it was agreed, under Germany's Chairmanship of the OSCE in 2016, that Chişinău and Tiraspol would first engage in direct talks to overcome a series of technical issues.[13] The reasoning behind this approach was that achieving some tangible benefits for the people on both banks of the Nistru River would increase trust between the conflicting parties.

The aim of improving the life of ordinary people was and is uncontroversial. Yet the Berlin Agreement, and a supplementary 2017 decision taken under the Austrian Chairmanship of the OSCE, which together have become known as the "Berlin Plus Package", have been criticized by Moldova's civil society and expert community. The Berlin Plus Package's agreements are faulted for entailing concessions to the separatists as well as a retreat from the initial goals of the

---

12 "On the meeting of mediators from Ukraine, the Russian Federation, and the OSCE with the representatives of the Republic of Moldova and Transdniestria", *OSCE*, n. d., https://www.osce.org/files/f/documents/7/9/16558.pdf.
13 J. Pieńkowski, "Renewal of Negotiations on Resolving the Transnistria Conflict", *PISM*, 19 December 2017, https://pism.pl/publications/Renewal_of_ Negotiations_on_Resolving_the_Transnistria_Conflict".

third basket.[14] The concrete issues addressed by the two agreements include the following:[15]

1. apostilles of diplomas issued in the Transnistrian region;
2. use of vehicles with number plates issued in Transnistria in international road traffic;
3. cooperation in the area of telecommunication;
4. protocols regarding cooperation in the area of meteorology and protection of natural resources in the Nistru River basin;
5. cooperation in the area of law enforcement, including exchange of updated lists of existing criminal cases;
6. the unhindered work of Latin-script schools in Transnistria;
7. access to agricultural land for the citizens of the Republic of Moldova who reside on the territory controlled by the constitutional authorities;[16]
8. freedom of movement between the two sides of people, goods, and services, in particular the opening of the Gura-Bicului Bridge.

As before, the Moldovan constitutional authorities have largely stuck to their commitments and approved the agreed legal and administrative documents to implement the agreements. For instance, documents issued by the Taras Shevchenko University of Tiraspol can now be authenticated in EU member states.[17] Vehicles from the left bank of the

---

14 "Protocol of the official meeting of the permanent conference for political questions in the framework of the negotiating process on the Transnistrian settlement", *OSCE*, n. d., https://www.osce.org/files/f/documents/d/f/244656.pdf.
15 "Măsuri de consolidare a încrederii: Pachetul 'Berlin-plus'", *OSCE*, n. d., https://www.osce.org/ro/mission-to-moldova/392477.
16 "Protocol of the official meeting of the permanent conference for political questions in the framework of the negotiating process on the Transnistrian settlement".
17 "407 diplomas of neutral model have been authenticated within 3 years from the implementation of the Protocol Decision of 25 November 2017", *Guvernul Republicii Moldova*, n. d., https://gov.md/en/content/407-diplomas-neutral-model-have-been-authenticated-within-3-years-implementation-protocol.

Nistru River have access to international road traffic by using neutral car plates issued by two Vehicle Registration Points in Rîbnița and Tiraspol.[18]

On the other side, Tiraspol has taken advantage of missing mechanisms for implementing some technical agreements, and has repeatedly postponed fulfilling its parts of the deal. Schools that use the Latin script in teaching in the Transnistrian region face constant pressure from the local authorities.[19] Farmers are denied access to their farmland in the separatist region.[20] Sometimes, additional check points along the administrative line and within the Security Zone are set up overnight.[21]

The original 1992 Moldovan-Russian "Agreement on the principles of a peaceful settlement of the armed conflict in the Transnistrian region of the Republic of Moldova" had already obliged the conflicting parties to avoid any impediments that would lead to restrictions of the movement of people, goods, and services. Yet the relevant Article 5 of the 1992 Agreement continues to be disregarded by the Transnistrian region's separatist authorities. Its contents constantly become subject to re-negotiation due to the setting up of illegal check points (both mobile and stationary) hindering free

---

18 "Law no.170/2018 on the registration of transport means and amendment of some legislative acts (in force since 1 September 2018)". *Guvernul Republicii Moldova*, n. d., https://gov.md/en/content/vehicle-registration-points-transnistri an-region-celebrate-two-years-functioning.
19 "Freedom in the World 2021, Transnistria", *Freedom House*, n. d., https://free domhouse.org/country/transnistria/freedom-world/2021.
20 I. Gulca, "Farmers from Dubasari district, double victims of Transnistrians and the pandemic". *Anticoruptie.md*, 25 March 2020, https://anticoruptie.md/ro/sp ecial/fermierii-din-raionul-dubasari-duble-victime-ale-transnistrenilor-si-ale-pa ndemiei.
21 D. Minzarari, "Moldova's Degrading Sovereignty Amid Coronavirus Spike", *The Jamestown Foundation*, 15 July 2020, https://jamestown.org/program/mol-dovas-degrading-sovereignty-amid-coronavirus-spike/.

movement.[22] Tiraspol's behavior increases public frustration on the right bank, and creates the impression that Moldova is merely making concessions in the negotiations.

As a result, the Berlin Plus Package's attempt to increase trust among partners and prepare an opening of the third basket, that is, a discussion of the political status of the Transnistrian region and the Russian military presence, has not been successful. The negotiations have become hostage to the myopic interests of the Transnistrian region leaders, backed by Russia. The strategy of "let's start with small technical steps to pave the way for a sustainable political settlement" has shown itself to be detrimental to conflict resolution. Instead, it has contributed to a strengthening of the Tiraspol regime and the flourishing of corrupt elites.

In retrospect, the 1997 Moscow Memorandum on the Bases for Normalization of Relations between the Republic of Moldova and Transnistria proved to be the wrong path.[23] Intending to achieve a quick political settlement of the conflict, it granted the self-proclaimed separatist authorities of the Transnistrian region the status of an equal party in the negotiations. Today, one must conclude that this fateful move a quarter of century ago inhibited rather than advanced the settlement process.

The resulting lack of sustainable results in settling the conflict has, over the years, proven the uselessness of the existing negotiations format and its resolution strategies. During the entire negotiation process more than 200 documents have been signed. Paradoxically, the majority of these

---

22 "Soglashenie o printsipakh mirnogo uregulirovaniia vooruzhennogo konflikta v Pridnevstrovskom regione Respubliki Moldova, ot 21 iiulia 1992 goda", *Guvernul Republicii Moldova*, n. d., https://gov.md/sites/default/files/1992-07-21-ru-moscow-agr_on_principles_of_peaceful_settlem.pdf.

23 "Moscow Memorandum on the Bases for Normalization of Relations between the Republic of Moldova and Transdneistria", *OSCE*, 8 May 1997, https://www.osce.org/files/f/documents/f/9/42309.pdf.

documents have, instead of bringing the parties closer together, created new impediments for a rapprochement and increased resentment on both sides of the Nistru River. The current format of negotiations legitimizes the self-proclaimed separatist authorities in the Transnistrian region, who often further the Kremlin's interests rather than those of the local population.

## The Role of the International Community

As one of the official mediators, the OSCE with its specific mandate and institutional limitations has often ended up legitimizing the Tiraspol regime. The desire of some leading Western OSCE nations to obtain positive results in the settlement of the conflict and, as much as possible, to avoid alienating Moscow has, most of the time, led to novel regulations favored by the secessionist regime. Obtaining such concessions from Chișinău—rather than fostering human rights in the separatist region and making both Tiraspol and Moscow accountable for their violations—has de facto become the main content and outcome of the negotiations, if one looks back on their record over the last 30 years.

The role of the EU and the US as observers in the negotiations is important in that the Transnistrian settlement, to a significant degree, depends on the engagement of the great powers. Yet Transnistrian conflict resolution is not a priority on the EU's and US's foreign agendas. The topic briefly attracted the interest of the EU in Angela Merkel's so-called Meseberg Process of 2010-2011. Resolution of the Transnistria conflict served as a critical test case for Russia when Germany and France were seeking to integrate Russia into a wider European security architecture. However, once the Meseberg Process proved to be leading nowhere, Western interest in Moldova's territorial conflict declined again.

Both the EU and the US have instead provided assistance to the Transnistrian region. The EU negotiated a tailored DCFTA for the region and has provided financial assistance via its Support to Confidence Building Measures Program, aimed at increasing trust between people on both sides of the Nistru River. However, no change in attitude on the part of the Transnistrian region's separatist leaders followed these efforts. Seeking to build confidence, Western assistance to the region, with no clear medium- and long-term strategy, tackles only small insubstantial issues. Sometimes, such help even strengthens the secessionist regime and supports its lack of accountability.

## The Main Positions in the Negotiations

The Moldovan government aims for the full reintegration of the country based on the 2005 Law No. 173 on the basic provisions of the special legal status of the localities on the left bank of the Nistru River (Transnistria).[24] The end goal expressed in this document is to provide the Transnistrian region with the status of an administrative-territorial entity within the Republic of Moldova, with the right to exercise its powers in accordance with and fully respecting the Constitution and laws of the Republic of Moldova. This also implies a complete withdrawal of Russian military units, the region's demilitarization, and its democratization. The restoration of Moldova's territorial integrity and sovereignty, as well as of the principle of a host nation's consent to the stationing of foreign troops on its territory, would also restore respect for international law and the key OSCE principles of the Helsinki Final Act as well as the Paris Charter.

---

24 "Law No. 173 on the basic provisions of the special legal status of the localities on the left bank of the Nistru River (Transnistria)", 22 July 2005, https://www.legis.md/cautare/getResults?doc_id=16014&lang=ro.

The separatist side, on the other hand, calls for far-reaching independence and the maintenance of a de facto self-functioning Russophone local administrative regime that identifies itself as the "Pridnestrovian Moldovan Republic" (Приднестровская Молдавская Республика [ПМР]). Currently, this pseudo-state functions independently of and isolated from Chişinău, which means that the constitutional authorities of the Republic of Moldova have limited leverage in the region. Moldova's external borders in the Transnistrian region are controlled with the support of Ukrainian partners, with whom common border control checkpoints have been set up.

During the decades-long negotiation process, two major resolution plans were presented to the conflicting parties. In November 2003, the Russian Federation put forward the "Kozak Memorandum", named after the official Russian negotiator and presumed Memorandum author, Dmitrii Kozak, then Deputy Head of the Presidential Administration of Russia. His Memorandum foresaw the creation of a "federation" in the Republic of Moldova. This scenario provided the Transnistrian region with its own state bodies and foresaw a blurry division of competences between the central authorities, on the one side, and the envisaged federal subjects, on the other. This asymmetric "federation" was supposed to have a Federal Parliament composed of two Houses — a Senate and a House of Representatives. The description of their practical functioning regarding the adoption of federal laws suggested an absolute veto right for Transnistria as a "subject of the federation". Among other gains, Transnistria's local leaders would have control over the foreign and security policies of the reintegrated Moldovan state. In practice, this would mean, for instance, that Moscow would be able to block Moldova's integration into the West, and especially into the EU and NATO. Moreover, though Kozak had initially stated that Russia would not employ troops during the conflict resolution process, other Russian officials later contradicted him. They spoke instead of a deployment of up to 2,000 "peacekeepers", armed with light weapons and helicopters, for a transition period until complete demilitarization.[25]

Chişinău's last-minute withdrawal from the signing of the Memorandum led to a freeze in relations between Moldova and Russia. In reaction, Moscow introduced several embargos on the import of Moldovan wine, fruits and vegetables. The aborted adoption of the Kozak Memorandum also meant the disgrace of Vladimir Voronin, the 2001-2009 communist president of Moldova, who lost Russia's political support.

The victory of the Orange Revolution in Ukraine and the election of the pro-Western politician Viktor Yushchenko as President in late 2004 changed the dynamics in Moldovan-Ukrainian relations. Previously, Ukraine had been seen as not fully supporting the reintegration policies of the Republic of Moldova. After Yushchenko's inauguration in early 2005, the new Ukrainian head of state offered the second major settlement road map. It became known as the "Yushchenko Plan" and envisaged the democratization as well as the demilitarization of Transnistria. Chişinău accepted the Ukrainian plan and proceeded with the implementation of its obligations. Thus, on July 22, 2005, the Moldovan Parliament adopted Law No. 173 on the basic provisions of the special legal status of the localities on the left bank of the Nistru River

---

25 I. Boţan, "Procesul de negocieri ca modalitate de amânare a soluţionăriiproblemei", *Moldova – Transnistria: Eforturi comune pentru un viitor prosper*, edited by Denis Matveev, Galina Şelari, Elena Bobkova, and Bianca Cseke (Chişinău: Editura Cu drag, 2009), 25.

(Transnistria).[26] Although this Law was met with reservations by the Transnistrian region's separatist leaders and the Russian Federation, its political repercussions led to two essential changes on the ground.

In November 2005, the European Union Border Assistance Mission to Moldova and Ukraine (EUBAM), based on an October 2005 Memorandum of Understanding signed by the European Commission and the Governments of Moldova and Ukraine, was launched. On March 1, 2006, Ukrainian Prime Minister Yuri Yekhanurov signed a government resolution stipulating that only goods that complied with the Republic of Moldova's customs legislation could cross the Ukrainian border from Transnistria. This step was not only undertaken to enhance Moldova's constitutional authorities' control over the customs service at the border. It was also to stop the smuggling of illegal goods from the Transnistrian region to Ukraine, mainly to the Port of Odessa, an important source of income for the Transnistrian political and business elites.

In Moldova, all political leaders since independence have adhered to the idea that a sustainable resolution means providing the Transnistrian region with a special legal status, as an administrative-territorial entity within the Republic of Moldova, i.e. some sort of "federalization" giving Tiraspol a degree of influence on Chișinău's political decision-making. However, the various government negotiations through the years have shown varying degrees of consistency in promoting the reintegration idea. There has been insufficient political will to take effective steps to attract the citizens of the Republic of Moldova residing in the Transnistrian region, on the

---

26 "Law No. 173 on the basic provisions of the special legal status of the localities on the left bank of the Nistru River (Transnistria)", 22 July 2005, https://www.legis.md/cautare/getResults?doc_id=16014&lang=ro.

one hand, and to face the challenges posed by the Russian Federation, on the other.

Moldova's political and systemic corruption, as well as its poverty and deficient socio-economic development, have preserved the status quo favored by several decision-makers in Tiraspol, Moscow, and, partly, Chișinău. For some, the Transnistrian region has become an uncontrollable space for the smuggling and trafficking of goods, people and ammunition. For other actors, the region in its current set-up represents a peculiar form of political capital. The region provides constant support for left-wing parties in Moldova's political spectrum. Even though the separatist leaders have always pleaded for independence, they encourage Transnistria's population to vote during national Moldovan elections, on the right bank of the Nistru River.

Moreover, Moldovan citizens in the Transnistrian region are being bribed to vote for specific parties and candidates, usually pro-Russian ones. Left-bank voters are transported to the polling stations on the right bank, and promised benefits for their votes.[27] For instance, 28,173 Moldovan citizens residing in the Transnistrian region cast their vote in Moldova's 2021 snap parliamentary elections. This was approximately twice the number of left-bank voters who took part in Moldova's 2020 national presidential elections. The very fact that the national elections attracted residents of the Transnistrian region, and led to their organized participation, illustrates the artificial nature of the Transnistrian separatist leaders' endeavor.

Fighting corruption on the Nistru's right bank was first publicly identified as a prerequisite for conflict resolution by

---

27 Transitions Online, "Transnistrian election fraud 'a slap in the face of Moldovan democracy'", *Global Voices*, 1 September 2021, https://globalvoices.org/2021/09/01/transnistrian-election-fraud-a-slap-in-the-face-of-moldovan-democracy/.

the new President of the Republic of Moldova, Maia Sandu. Elected in 2020, she proposed the adoption of a broadly agreed political settlement document in which the sovereignty and integrity of the country would be respected, and which would secure the future unified state's functionality. Sandu is thus returning to an approach that seeks fundamental conflict settlement rather than one that merely tackles technical issues in small steps, the strategy for many years.[28]

## The Russian Federation: Frenemy or Adversary?

Despite some observers' view that Russia's interest in the Transnistrian region is decreasing, Moscow continues to send messages hinting at potential conflict escalation should serious steps towards the eviction of the Russian military, and Moldova's integration into Western security structures, start to happen. The strange role of the Russian Federation within the conflict settlement process derives from its double incarnation. It is supposed to be a mediator between the conflicting parties, on the one hand, but is the crucial supporter of the separatists, if not an actual aggressor against the Moldovan state, on the other.

According to the 1992 Ceasefire Agreement, Russia was assigned a prominent role in the so-called Joint Control Commission (JCC).[29] The tripartite JCC consists of representatives from Moldova, Russia and the Transnistrian region and has its headquarters in Tighina/Bender, a city with a special

---

28 "Participation of Maia Sandu, President of the Republic of Moldova at the talk show 'Moldova in Direct'", *National Moldovan Broadcaster – Moldova 1*, 3 June 2021, https://www.youtube.com/watch?v=G8HaitDUflY.
29 "Agreement between Republic of Moldova and the Russian Federation on the principles of a peaceful settlement of the armed conflict in the Transnistrian region of the Republic of Moldova", https://gov.md/sites/default/files/1992-07-21-ru-moscow-agr_on_principles_of_peaceful_settlem.pdf.

security regime.³⁰ According to article 3 of the 1992 Agreement, all parties included in JCC should provide military contingents which, along with the Transnistrian separatists' "police", ensure public order in Tighina/Bender. The JCC's mandate is to monitor the implementation of the ceasefire agreement and restore peace, to preserve law and order, particularly on the territory of the established demilitarized Security Zone, and to coordinate the operational activity of the peacekeeping mission under the Trilateral Joint Military Command.³¹ Today, the overall peacekeeping contingent consists of 375 people from the Russian Federation, 296 from Moldova, and 336 from the Transnistrian region. There are also 10 military observers from Ukraine.

However, the JCC has not managed to fully implement its mandate due to disagreements and lack of consensus between the three delegations. There are also continuous violations of the Security Zone regime by the Transnistrian region's troops and the Russian contingent stationed on the territory of the Republic of Moldova. The most severe violations are:

1. A sharp increase in the number of the Transnistrian local authorities' so-called "border guards" in the Security Zone, who hinder the free movement of goods and people—an issue that constantly fails to reach the official negotiation agenda as Russian Federation delegates continue to invoke the need for additional information;
2. Cases of abductions of people and their illegal imprisonment;

---

30 Tiraspol is the capital and largest city in the Transnistrian region.
31 "The peacekeeping mission consisted initially of 5 Russian, 3 Moldovan and 2 Transdniestrian battalions. According to the Odessa Agreement signed on August 20, 1998, the number of peacekeepers was decreased to 500 each", *OSCE*, https://www.osce.org/files/f/documents/6/d/42310.pdf.

3. Joint military exercises by the so-called Operative Group of Russian Forces (OGRF) together with Tiraspol's semi-regular troops.

Russia's de facto aggressor role in Moldova is associated with both its destructive involvement in the incipient phase of the conflict in 1992, and the maintenance of a regular military detachment and ammunition depot on the territory of the Republic of Moldova since then. According to article 4 of the 1992 Agreement, "[t]he contingents of the 14th Army of the Russian Federation stationing in the Republic of Moldova will strongly observe neutrality. [...] Questions regarding their status and conditions for step by step withdrawal will be agreed in the framework of the Republic of Moldova and Russian Federation dialogue".[32]

When discussing Russian troops on the territory of the Republic of Moldova, one must distinguish between the "peacekeeping forces" provided by the Russian Federation, present in the country according to the 1992 ceasefire agreement, and the so-called Operative Group of Russian Forces (OGRF) in Cobasna. Approximately 1,500 Russian soldiers are stationed in Cobasna to safeguard 20,000 tons of ammunition. The Cobasna ammunition depot was set up in the 1940s. During the Soviet period, artillery ammunition depot No. 1411 was a strategic arsenal of the western military district of the USSR. The continued presence of the so-called OGRF on Moldova's territory is illegal. In addition, it violates the country's explicitly neutral status as declared in the

---

32 "Agreement between Republic of Moldova and the Russian Federation on the principles of a peaceful settlement of the armed conflict in the Transnistrian region of the Republic of Moldova", https://gov.md/sites/default/files/1992-07-21-ru-moscow-agr_on_principles_of_peaceful_settlem.pdf.

Moldovan Constitution adopted in 1994 and also the principle of the host state's consent to the stationing of foreign troops.[33]

With regard to the Russian peacekeeping detachment, Chișinău suggests transforming it into a strictly civilian and humanitarian monitoring mission with an international mandate and as part of a multinational contingent. Regarding the so-called OGRF, Moldova pleads for an immediate withdrawal of the troops and munitions stationed illegally on its territory. The so-called OGRF practically represents a segment of the 14th Russian Army troops, which were reorganized in July 1995. The Transnistrian separatist leaders, as well as Moscow, manipulate the numbers of these troops and the arguments justifying their presence. Since the beginning of the conflict, the main functions of the so-called OGRF, as of its predecessor, have been to provide technical and training support, military supplies, and equipment to the breakaway region. Today, most of the contingent's personnel has been enrolled from the region's local residents, who are either already Russian Federation citizens or who will receive Russian citizenship.

Russia invokes the need to maintain the so-called OGRF so as to ensure the rotation of the Russian peacekeeper contingent and provide security to the ammunition depot. In 1994, Russia signed an agreement with Moldova envisaging the withdrawal of its military contingent from Transnistria, but made it conditional upon a political settlement of the conflict and the setting up of a special status for the Transnistrian region within Moldova. It thus depends on the

---

33 Paragraph 14 of the OSCE 1994 Code of Conduct on Politico-Military Aspects of Security (https://www.osce.org/files/f/documents/5/7/41355.pdf) stipulates that the stationing of armed forces on the territory of participating States is only possible "in accordance with their freely negotiated agreement as well as in accordance with international law".

implementation of the same third basket whose realization has been consistently sabotaged by Moscow over the years.

Important additional provisions were made in the November 1999 OSCE Istanbul Summit Declaration. The document's Article 19 says:

> Recalling the decisions of the Budapest and Lisbon Summits and Oslo Ministerial Meeting, we reiterate our expectation of an early, orderly and complete withdrawal of Russian troops from Moldova. In this context, we welcome the recent progress achieved in the removal and destruction of the Russian military equipment stockpiled in the Trans-Dniestrian region of Moldova and the completion of the destruction of non-transportable ammunition. We welcome the commitment by the Russian Federation to complete withdrawal of the Russian forces from the territory of Moldova by the end of 2002. We also welcome the willingness of the Republic of Moldova and of the OSCE to facilitate this process, within their respective abilities, by the agreed deadline.[34]

## The Ammunition Depot at Cobasna: A Way Out or a Stalemate?

The 1999 OSCE Istanbul Document linked the withdrawal and destruction of Russian ammunitions stored in the Transnistrian region to the adapted Conventional Armed Forces in Europe (CFE) treaty, as Moscow committed to destroy or remove all CFE-relevant materials.[35] Russia's fulfillment of the Istanbul commitments would open up a ratification of the CFE treaty and its entry into force. The OSCE Mission in Moldova had its mandate expanded "in terms of ensuring transparency of the removal and destruction of Russian ammunition and armaments and co-ordination of financial and technical assistance offered to facilitate withdrawal and

---

[34] "Istanbul Document 1999", *OSCE*, n. d., https://www.osce.org/files/f/documents/6/5/39569.pdf, 49-50.

[35] "Agreement on adaptation of the Treaty on Conventional Armed Forces in Europe", *OSCE*, 19 November 1999, https://www.osce.org/files/f/documents/e/3/14108.pdf.

destruction".[36] A voluntary fund was established and equipment provided by the OSCE. Thus, the first part of the deal was being fulfilled.

The second part of the deal was, however, postponed due to the reluctance of the Transnistrian leaders to comply with it; more importantly, Russia was having second thoughts about the deal. The 2002 Porto OSCE Ministerial Council not only agreed with Moscow's reservations, but also adopted a statement whose formulation later hindered finalization of the withdrawal: "We welcome the Russian Federation's commitment to complete the withdrawal of Russian forces as early as possible and its intention to do so by 31 December 2003, *provided necessary conditions are in place*".[37] No specification of these "necessary conditions" was provided. This was also the last time that an OSCE Ministerial could agree on a declaration, as Russia would veto all formulations not to its liking.

It is true that, between 2001 and 2003, the OSCE did facilitate Russia's withdrawal of more than 20,000 tons of ammunition and weapons, falling under the CFE Treaty, from the Cobasna depot. However, another 20,000 tons of Russian ammunition remain on Moldovan soil. In 2007, Russia suspended implementation of the CFE Treaty stating: "The treaty, signed at the time of the Cold War, has ceased to respond to modern European realities and to meet our security interests. [...] [NATO member states] have taken a number of steps that are incompatible with the spirit and the letter of the treaty".[38] The suspension of the CFE Treaty as well as the unfortunate Porto statement diminished the ability to maneuver

---

36 "Permanent Council, Decision No. 329, PC.DEC/329", *OSCE*, 9 December 1999.
37 "Tenth Meeting of the Ministerial Council 6 and 7 December 2002", *OSCE*, n. d., https://www.osce.org/files/f/documents/b/f/40521.pdf, italics added.
38 "Russia Suspends Participation in CFE Treaty", *Radio Free Europe*, 12 December 2007, https://www.rferl.org/a/1079256.html.

in implementing the Istanbul commitments and left the withdrawal of the remaining military contingent and ammunition to Moscow's whim. Following the visit of the Russian Minister of Defense Sergei Shoigu to Chișinău in August 2019, Moscow signaled its readiness to start talks on ammunition destruction. However, no concrete steps have been taken since. In 2019, at a joint press conference with Moldova's new Foreign and European Integration Minister Nicu Popescu, the Russian Minister of Foreign Affairs Sergey Lavrov stated:

> Considering the security aspects, Defence Minister Shoigu suggested disposing of the ammunition whose term of storage has expired. We have talked to our colleagues about the actions that are required for this. It is necessary to deliver the relevant equipment, dispatch specialists, determine a source of funding, and then sign a contract. All these steps must obey the security standards existing in the Russian Armed Forces. This is the only way. Preparations for this will take slightly more than a year. The militaries on both sides must contact each other in order to resolve everything on paper and plan the specific process. We are ready for these contacts.[39]

The continuing presence of the so-called OGRF on Moldovan soil can be explained by its strategic importance for Moscow. It marks the Kremlin's continued interest in the region, and secures Russian presence at the Moldovan-Ukrainian border. At that same press conference, the Russian Foreign Minister said:

> The Russian Group of Forces deployed in Transnistria, where the 14th Army was stationed, and the Joint Peacekeeping Force that also includes Russian military are very important components of peace that has persisted in the region after the Russian military stopped the bloodshed there 25 years ago. Not a single shot has been fired since then. It is perfectly obvious that this is an inalienable part of the efforts we are pursuing to settle the Transnistrian

---

39 "Foreign Minister Sergey Lavrov's statement and answers to media questions at a joint news conference following his talks with Minister of Foreign Affairs and European Integration of Moldova Nicu Popescu", *The Ministry of Foreign Affairs of the Russian Federation,* 11 September 2019, https://www.mid.ru/en/posledniye_dobavlnenniye/-/asset_publisher/MCZ7HQuMdqBY/content/id/3782852.

problem, with account taken of the territorial integrity of Moldova, a neutral Moldova, and Transnistria's special status.[40]

## Conclusions and Recommendations

The resolution of the Transnistrian conflict requires will and commitment from all the actors involved, and in particular a fundamental reorientation of Moscow's approach to the region. In addition, the Moldovan constitutional authorities need to demonstrate greater ownership than hitherto of the reintegration process. In this respect, the following changes and policies are recommended:

*To Moldova's government and parliament:*

1. Moldova's authorities should formulate a comprehensive, clear, thematically focused, and financially backed reintegration strategy based on already existing international commitments and on the European association agenda. A viable solution to the Transnistrian conflict requires a unified position or "untouchable consensus" of the political class in Moldova, independent of ideology, a position based on the principles of independence, sovereignty, and the territorial integrity of Moldova and not on geopolitical preferences.
2. Knowledge about the Transnistrian conflict on both banks of the Nistru River is inadequate. Though the Transnistrian conflict heavily impacts the development of the entire Moldovan state, the topic is insufficiently prominent among politicians and the larger public. People on both banks of the Nistru River do not yet associate the conflict's settlement with a more successful and sustainable socio-economic development of the country. The Transnistrian issue should thus be made open to the larger public and presented as a challenge to national security. All parties should be encouraged to get involved in conflict resolution, to

---

40 Ibid.

speak out more. Information that avoids abstruse technicalities should be offered.
3. Moldova's National Public Broadcaster should develop an editorial policy promoting societal reconciliation and unification, offering consistently truthful information, and identifying red lines. Training and education of journalists on the ethical standards of conflict resolution should be provided to allow them to communicate more professionally on such issues. The Audio-Visual Council of Moldova should set norms and regulations addressing the coverage of the Transnistrian conflict settlement, in cooperation with the Bureau for Reintegration.
4. The Republic of Moldova should develop a unified position on the role of the Russian Federation in the settlement process. The hitherto prevalent hesitant approach has not only made dialogue with the Russian Federation more difficult in general, but has also allowed the intensification of existing problematic and controversial issues in such fields as socio-economic and trade relations, energy, security, etc.
5. The Republic of Moldova's authorities should intensify cooperation with their Ukrainian counterparts as well as elaborate a common position/view on regional security architecture, bearing in mind both countries' EU accession aspirations. Mirror activities at the level of civil society could be undertaken, thus increasing knowledge about each other and building bridges between institutions, civil society organizations and the media environment.

*To international organizations and foreign actors:*

1. Under the OSCE umbrella, more clarity needs to be achieved regarding the issue of the Russian military presence in Moldova so as to avoid manipulation and disinformation. The OSCE should take into account the Moldovan request for a monitoring mission in the Security Zone comprised of international experts under the OSCE umbrella. Restoration of respect for international law and OSCE principles (as laid out in the Helsinki Final Act and Paris Charter) and commitments should underlie all OSCE efforts.

2. The 5+2 negotiation format stakeholders should develop mechanisms guaranteeing the execution of the agreed provisions, as well as penalties for slowing down or jeopardizing implementation of the agreed commitments. Considering the largely unsuccessful conflict resolution attempts over the years, and the lack of sustainable progress, withdrawal of Russian troops and ammunition should be requested as a precondition for further talks.
3. The EU and the US should put the Transnistrian conflict higher on their foreign policy agendas in relation to other protracted conflicts in Russia's neighborhood, include it in their bilateral dialogue with Russia, and hold Moscow accountable for its violations of international law in general, as well as of OSCE principles and commitments in particular.
4. The EU and the US should use financial assistance as well as instruments under the Association Agreement, including the DCFTA, for making the Transnistrian region's authorities more accountable and respectful of human rights and freedoms, as well as to initiate reforms that would foster reintegration. Such assistance should be closely coordinated with the Republic of Moldova's authorities and reintegration plans.
5. The EU should review the effectiveness of its Confidence Building Measures, and align its institutional support to promoting reunification. The EU should consider reviving its practice of having a Special Representative for Moldova, i.e. a person dedicated particularly to the solution of the Transnistrian conflict. A similar special representative for Moldova from the US would also be beneficial.
6. The OSCE, as well as Ukraine, the EU and the US, should pay greater attention and commit resources to unveiling corruption schemes linked to the separatist regime as well as other uses of the Transnistrian region for illegal activities.
7. The EU and its member states, the US and the international organizations present in the Republic of Moldova should continue to refrain from taking unilateral decisions related

to the Transnistrian region without consultation with and the consent of Moldova's constitutional authorities. Such actions would not only hinder conflict resolution but could also contribute to a deepening of the conflict.

*Victoria Roşa is a Foreign Affairs and Security Expert as well as Member of the Board of the Foreign Policy Association of Moldova, and former Security and Defense Advisor to the Prime Minister of the Republic of Moldova.*

# Georgia and the Russian Occupation

*Diana Janse*

DOI: https://doi.org/10.24216/9783838216881_005

## Executive Summary

*For the past three decades, Russia has been systematically instrumentalizing Georgia's non-government-controlled areas to promote Russia's own geopolitical agenda; in essence, to impede Georgia's escape from Russia'ssphere of influence, to prevent Georgia from making its own security choices and to maintain a military foothold in the region. The international response to Georgia's conflict regions was inadequate from the start. Russia's influence and leverage in the non-government-controlled areas have been amplified by the various monitoring and peacekeeping arrangements put in place at the end of these conflicts, and this influence and leverage have been not only tolerated but blessed by the international community in breach of the key principles of effective conflict resolution – neutrality and maintaining the trust of both conflicting parties. In this way, the international community has left the issue of Georgia's territorial integrity in the hands of Russia. The fact that Russia was allowed to play mediator and "peacekeeper" while also being a party to the conflicts with its own interests has been ignored over the years, and many countries have partly or fully bought into the Russianmediator narrative. In the years building up to the 2008 war, the prevailing perception fomented by Russia was that the conflicts concerning Abkhazia and South Ossetia were primarily between the secessionist regions and Tbilisi. While this aspect of the conflicts is genuine, Russia's critical role in supporting the breakaway regions politically, economically and militarily, and in undermining Georgian efforts at confidence building were consistently downplayed or even completely ignored. This unwillingness to highlight Russia's* role in the conflicts, and its violations of international law and agreed principles and commitments continued after the 2008 war. At the same time, Russia's use of military force in the war further enhanced the country's military presence in the region at the expense of Georgia's territorial integrity. Georgia's territory's integrity should be considered part of a wider European peace and security agenda. The weak international response to Russian actions before, during and after the 2008 war – and to Russia's subsequent non-adherence to the six-point plan in particular – has continued to undermine not only Georgia's territorial integrity but also European peace and security. If the West is serious about defending a rules-based international order, it should put Georgia back on the international agenda, consistently call out Russia's role in perpetuating the Georgian conflicts and put in place a holistic containment policy vis-à-vis Russia. Furthermore, it needs to step up its support for Georgia's fragile democracy, increase its presence in Georgia and support Georgia's ability to defend its sovereignty against further external aggression. In addition, the West should support Georgia's reconciliation efforts with the regions and find ways to break the isolation of the people in the non-government-controlled areas. The final chapters of conflict resolution in Georgia are still to be written. The conclusions that Brussels and Washington draw from the weak response to Russia's action before, during and after the war in 2008, and on the continuing policies of Russian aggression in Georgia, in Ukraine and elsewhere, still matter.

## Introduction

More than 30 years after regaining independence, Georgia is still struggling for control over all of its internationally recognized territory. The Georgian breakaway regions of Abkhazia and the Tskhinvali region are de facto occupied by Russia, although Russia denies any involvement in the conflicts and has recognized the breakaway regions as independent states.

This paper discusses what can be done to restore Georgia's territorial integrity. It provides an overview of the recent history of the conflicts and the various conflict resolution designs, assessing the weaknesses and relevance of the latter given the current realities. It touches on the current relationships between Tbilisi and Sukhumi, and between Tbilisi and Tskhinvali — and on Georgia's relationship with Russia.

## Background

Georgia's two conflict regions have their own distinct histories and dynamics. Relations between the non-government-controlled areas, on the one hand, and the Georgian central government, on the other, are complicated but also different. The non-government-controlled areas are also different in their ethnic composition, and both areas enjoyed a degree of autonomy in Soviet times.

As the Soviet Union was in the process of breaking apart, the local minority elites in Sukhumi and Tskhinvali feared the loss of their standing, power and privileges in a newly independent Georgia. Nationalistic and xenophobic sentiments ran high and Georgia's then president, Zviad Gamsakhurdia, was calling for a Georgia for the (ethnic) Georgians. The spark of conflict, however, ignited in 1990, just before independence, when the local South Ossetian district administration in Tskhinvali declared a separate republic within the Soviet Union, and its aspiration to unite with the republic of North Ossetia on the Russian side of the Caucasian mountains. At the time, the Tskhinvali region comprised about one-third ethnic Georgians and two-thirds ethnic Ossetians.

In response, the Georgian Parliament revoked South Ossetia's autonomous status within Georgia and sent in poorly trained Georgian armed forces. A South Ossetian militia managed to fight back, supported by the Russian army and militia from North Ossetia. A ceasefire agreement was signed that halted hostilities in July 1992 and final status talks were initiated. This short conflict resulted in thousands of casualties and some 10,000 refugees and internally displaced persons (IDPs) — the refugees fled north to Russia, the IDPs south to the rest of Georgia.

In Abkhazia, the war started later and ended with an even more devastating outcome for the Georgian central government. In the region at the time, the ethnic Abkhaz minority comprised some 20 percent of the population, while the ethnic Georgian population amounted to nearly 50 percent. The local Abkhaz political elite foresaw the decline of its influence in the local capital, Sukhumi, with Georgia's exit from the Soviet Union, a fear fueled by President Gamsakhurdia's unchecked nationalistic rhetoric. In January 1992, however, Gamsakhurdia was deposed by a military council in Tbilisi, which invited Eduard Shevardnadze to form a new government. Gamsakhurdia fled into exile. At this time of political turmoil in Tbilisi, the Abkhaz seized the chance to push for independence, just as the South Ossetians had. In the summer of 1992. The Georgian Minister of Defense launched an unauthorized attack on Abkhazia. Georgian troops and paramilitary forces marched into the separatist province and Sukhumi. Although initially successful, they were unable to hold onto their positions for long, as Russian military troops were sent in to back the Abkhaz. An ugly and devastating war followed and, by the end of 1993, Abkhaz forces, supported by Russian forces and militias from the North Caucasus, had pushed the Georgian forces back.

The final battle came after Shevardnadze, seeking to the end the war, agreed to withdraw Georgian troops from Sukhumi in return for a ceasefire. The truce was violated by the Abkhaz, however, who saw an opportunity to overrun the remaining Georgian positions. The Georgian forces were pushed back to the Enguri River, which divides Abkhazia from Georgia proper, a position that was maintained until the war of August 2008. (The exception was the Upper Kodori valley, which remained under the control of the local warlord Emzar Kvitsiani until the Georgian central government took control of it in 2006. It held on to it until August 2008.) The defeat led to the expulsion of the legitimate regional government, and of some 230,000 ethnic Georgians living in Abkhazia who have not yet been allowed to return.

## Conflict Resolution in Abkhazia

In Abkhazia, a first ceasefire agreement was reached in Moscow on September 3, 1992 by the Georgian central government, the de facto Abkhaz leadership and Russia. The agreement stipulated that "the territorial integrity of the Republic of Georgia shall be ensured", but it was never fully implemented. The ceasefire collapsed in October and fighting resumed.

In the coming months, the United Nations sought to revive the peace process, consulting with the OSCE and appointing a Special Envoy for Georgia. In July 1993, a new agreement was concluded between the Georgian central government and the de facto Abkhaz authorities; a new ceasefire was established and there was an agreement to deploy international observers. Shortly afterwards, UN Security Council resolution 858 (1993) established the United Nations Observer Mission in Georgia (UNOMIG), with up to 88 military observers tasked with verifying compliance with the ceasefire agreement. However, the ceasefire broke down again after Abkhaz forces, supported by the Russian military, attacked Sukhumi and other cities. By the end of September 1993, Abkhaz forces supported by Russia had taken control of all of Akbhazia apart from the Upper Kodori valley. UNOMIG's mission was partly suspended.

After UNOMIG's original mandate was invalidated by the fighting in Abkhazia, the UN launched various initiatives. In Moscow in May 1994, the UN Special Envoy joined the Georgian and Abkhaz sides in signing an "Agreement on a Ceasefire and Separation of Forces". Most notably, the parties agreed to the deployment of a peacekeeping force from the Commonwealth of Independent States (CIS) to monitor compliance with the agreement. In reality, however, the CIS peacekeeping force was a Russian one as no other CIS member state participated. Eventually, in 2002, the CIS meetings even dropped discussion of this operation and the vote to prolong its mandate, for which Russia had never bothered to seek approval in the first place.[1] Interestingly, the UN Security Council routinely continues to compliment a "CIS collective peacekeeping operation" in its UNOMIG resolutions.[2]

Given Russia's involvement in the conflict on the Abkhaz side, the agreement was in breach of the cardinal principles of effective conflict resolution and peacekeeping—the principles that a peacekeeping force must be neutral and that it must enjoy the trust of both sides. Instead, the West seemed to place its hopes in the then Western-leaning Russian Foreign Minister, Andrei Kozyrev, and the erratic Russian President, Boris Yeltsin. UNOMIG was tasked with monitoring the implementation of the agreement and observing the operation of the CIS force. Shortly afterwards, UNOMIG's observer force was scaled-up and its mandate expanded accordingly.

---

1 Vladimir Socor, "RUSSIA'S STRANGE 'PEACEKEEPING' OPERATION IN ABKHAZIA", *Jamestown Foundation,* May 5, 2008, available at https://jamestown.org/program/russias-strange-peacekeeping-operation-in-abkhazia.

2 United Nations Observer Mission in Georgia, available at: https://peacekeeping.un.org/mission/past/unomig/unomigDrs.htm.

## Conflict Resolution in South Ossetia

South Ossetia's war also ended with a ceasefire agreement, the Sochi Agreement, reached in the summer of 1992. At that time, Tbilisi had control over significant parts of the former autonomous *oblast*, including ethnic Georgian and mixed villages to the north of Tskhinvali, in the west and in the Akhalgori valley in the east. The agreement was brokered by Russia and signed by Yeltsin and the then Head of Parliament and later President of Georgia, Eduard Shevardnadze. The agreement defined a zone of conflict around Tskhinvali and established a security corridor along the southern part of the former administrative boundary of the de jure abolished South Ossetian autonomous *oblast*. As part of the agreement, a Joint Control Commission for Georgian-Ossetian Conflict Resolution (JCC) was set up with the clearly unbalanced participation of Georgian, South Ossetian, Russian and (Russian) North Ossetian representatives. This operated in South Ossetia and oversaw a Joint Peacekeeping Force (JPKF) of one battalion of Russian forces, one battalion of (Russian) North Ossetian forces and one Georgian battalion, all under Russian command. In reality, South Ossetian militias served as the North Ossetian force. The JPKF's activities were mainly concentrated in Tskhinvali and a 15-km radius around the city. Once again, the cardinal principles of effective conflict resolution and peacekeeping—neutrality and trust—were violated.

While the UN was more or less absent from the South Ossetian conflict resolution process, the OSCE did agree to monitor the ceasefire and to facilitate negotiations and a broader political framework for conflict resolution.

In summary, as a result of the two separatist wars in Georgia, in two separate sets of arrangements, one with the UN and the other with the OSCE, the West allowed Russia—

which had been supporting the separatists in both conflicts — to be the main peacekeeping force on the ground in both Abkhazia and the Tskhinvali region. At the same time, Russia maintained its power to veto any decision that ran contrary to its interests in the UN or the OSCE in relation to its role or engagement in the conflicts.

## Russian Peacekeeping or "Piece-keeping"?

In the more than ten years after the agreements and cessation of hostilities, no progress occurred on conflict settlement. A major factor was Russia's dual role, acting as peacekeeper, on the one hand, and negotiator, on the other, while supporting the secessionist leaderships in Tskhinvali and Sukhumi politically, economically and militarily. As the dust settled and the years passed, it became obvious that existing international involvement and mechanisms on the ground were inadequate and ill-designed for keeping the peace, let alone resolving the conflicts.

Instead, the UN mission in Abkhazia and its sister OSCE mission in the Tskhinvali region, paired with the Russian-led and Russia-dominated peacekeeping missions, were effectively being used by Russia as a tool for its own goals. Some of these goals — to keep the former Soviet republics within the Russian sphere of influence and prevent them from making their own security policy choices, and to maintain a military foothold in the region — also became more pronounced as Russia recovered from the turbulent 1990s and openly sought to regain its lost status and influence.

Nevertheless, there was little or no willingness in the international community to call Moscow to account for its abuses of this flawed peacekeeping design. Instead, the West regularly extended arrangements that allowed and made it easier for Moscow to block any initiative it did not like.

Russian peacekeeping turned into Russian "piece-keeping", in what was seen as its sphere of influence — in conflict with both UN and OSCE principles. This was true in the chaotic 1990s and continued to be the case as Russia slowly but steadily steered towards a more authoritarian path under President Putin.

Instead of turning up the pressure on Moscow to stop actively funding, fueling and supporting the separatists, however, much of West's attention turned to Tbilisi. After the Rose Revolution in 2003, Georgia quickly went from a failed state at the periphery of the former Soviet Union to a partner of the West, with a Western-oriented policy that sought both NATO and EU membership. The message to Tbilisi was that Georgia had to confront — and try to heal — the wounds of the wars and the underlying causes of ethnic Abkhaz' and ethnic Ossetians' distrust in Tbilisi. Although difficult, Georgia had to try to overcome separatist aspirations in Tskhinvali and Sukhumi with a compelling vision of a future for all of Georgia's peoples.

This was also an important aspect of the conflict resolution equation. The ethnic Abkhaz feared the return of the many ethnic Georgians who had fled during the war, which would make the Abkhaz a minority in their own region once again. Not all of the scars from the war had healed. Most ethnic Abkhaz sought independence but, if given the choice, would prefer Russian to Georgian dominance. The Abkhaz elite and the civil society activists participating in roundtables, Track 2 conferences or other similar dialogue initiatives were generally pro-Russian, and to a large extent funded by Russia and carrying Russian passports (circumstances meant that there were few real alternatives). Above all, they wanted to have a say in their own future.

In the smaller Tskhinvali region, things were different. The wounds from the war were not as deep as the conflict had not been as disastrous, the ethnic composition looked different and Georgians and Ossetians still lived side by side in some areas. Large parts of the area were under the control of Tbilisi, and even in other locations people could move back and forth to trade, enjoy state services provided by Tbilisi and visit relatives. In addition, the population shrank more and more as many moved to Russia or to Tbilisi from a region that had few prospects.

## The 2008 War

Hostilities between Russia and Georgia around the Georgian breakaway regions had been mounting for years prior to the 2008 war. Tensions between Sukhumi and Tbilisi, and between Tskhinvali and Tbilisi, were also high at times. Russia conducted military strikes against Georgia on two separate occasions in 2007.[3] Elsewhere, 2008 was an eventful year in the international arena. In February, Kosovo declared independence followed by a string of recognitions from Western states. In March, Russia unilaterally withdrew from the CIS sanctions regime against Abkhazia. In April, the possibility of Membership Action Plans (MAPs) for Georgia and Ukraine was discussed at the NATO Summit in Bucharest. The summit could not agree on MAPs, but paragraph 23 of the Summit Declaration welcomed "Ukraine's and Georgia's Euro-Atlantic aspirations for membership" and agreed "that these countries will become members of NATO".

In March 2008, Georgia withdrew from the JCC and demanded that a new formula be created, one that included the

---

3   J. Engvall, "OSCE and Military Confidence-Building in Crisis: Lessons from Georgia and Ukraine", https://www.foi.se/rapportsammanfattning?reportNo=FOI-R--4750--SE

European Union, the OSCE and the Sanakoev administration, that is, representatives from the Tskhinvali region who were favorable to Tbilisi. At the same time, command of the Georgian peacekeeping battalion in the Tskhinvali region was transferred to the Georgian Ministry of Defense.

In the spring of 2008, tensions increased, particularly in and around Abkhazia. Russia intensified its military activity and, without notifying Georgia or any international body, reinforced its forces by sending additional troops with heavy equipment. Georgia for its part increased its military presence near Abkhazia, which included unmanned aerial vehicles (UAVs). In April, a Russian fighter aircraft downed a Georgian reconnaissance UAV over Abkhazia. The incident was investigated by UNOMIG, which concluded that both parties were in violation of the 1994 Moscow Agreement on a Ceasefire and Separation of Forces.

Escalation continued. In May, despite Georgian protests, Russia sent a railway unit of approximately 400 troops to repair the Abkhaz railway. Work concluded a week before the war. As the summer arrived, tensions shifted from Abkhazia to the Tskhinvali region following numerous skirmishes between Georgian and separatist forces. In July, Russia began its Kavkaz 2008 military exercise in the North Caucasus military district, across the border from Georgia. In Tbilisi, the Georgian government accused Russia of using the exercise to conceal Russian mobilization along the Georgian border. Russian and Western analysts also saw the exercise as a rehearsal for a military operation in the region. According to official numbers, the drill involved 8,000 troops, 700 combat vehicles and more than 30 aircraft and helicopters.

In the Tskhinvali region, OSCE monitors on the ground had been documenting increased tensions for months by the summer of 2008. On August 4, an OSCE spot report informed the organization's participating states about exchanges of small arms fire and mortar shelling in what the report described as the most serious outbreak of firing since 2004. Similar incidents provided early warning in the run-up to the war, but nothing on which the OSCE could act.

By early August, Georgia blamed Russia for supporting the illegal separatist authorities and armed groups shelling Georgia from Tskhinvali. In the UN, the Georgian representative labeled events a calculated provocation to escalate the situation in order to justify a premeditated Russian military intervention.[4] For its part, Russia blamed Georgian armed forces for blatant and aggressive actions against the Tskhinvali region.

As the war began on August 8, several of the units participating in Kavkaz were redeployed to the war. However, numerous reports indicate that by that time, Russia's 58th Army was already inside Georgian territory. Hostilities quickly spread to areas beyond the zone of the Georgian-Ossetian conflict. When, on August 10, the UN Assistant Secretary-General for Peacekeeping Operations briefed the Security Council on events related to UNOMIG's mandate, he noted a military build-up of both Abkhaz and Russian forces on the Abkhaz side of the zone of conflict, as well as bombings of the Upper Kodori Valley. He reported that, as a result, UNOMIG had been forced to scale down its operations to essential patrols only. In the same briefing, the Georgian delegate described that an armed invasion by Russian troops had transformed into a full-scale occupation of parts of Georgian territory, while all Georgian troops had been withdrawn from the conflict zone.

---

4 https://www.un.org/en/sc/repertoire/2008-2009/Part%20I/Europe/08-09_Georgia.pdf.

Russia, for its part, argued that additional troops had been sent to Georgia to reinforce its peacekeepers and defend civilians, in order to prevent an ongoing "genocide" in the Tskhinvali region, removing Georgia from it. Russia also claimed the right to defend its own citizens, who were plentiful in the region following its campaign of handing out Russian passports.

Hostilities expanded in both intensity and geographical scope. Repeated international calls were made for a political solution to the conflict to restore the situation that prevailed prior to August 6. Many in the Security Council supported initiatives by France, which had then assumed the rotating presidency of the European Union, as well as international mediation efforts.

On August 11, 2008, the Security Council met in private in response to a request by Georgia. At the same time, France's president, Nicolas Sarkozy, mediated a six-point deal to defuse the conflict between Russia and Georgia and end the fighting. After some back and forth, a plan was agreed between Russia's President Dmitry Medvedev and Georgia's President Mikheil Saakashvili on August 12.

Some small differences existed between the French and Russian versions of the agreement, but the six principles in the deal were: (a) no recourse to the use of force; (b) the definitive cessation of (all) hostilities; (c) free access to humanitarian aid; (d) the withdrawal of Georgian forces to their places of permanent/usual deployment; (e) the withdrawal of Russian military forces to the line(s)[5] that existed prior to the outbreak of hostilities; and (f) the opening of international discussions on lasting security for Abkhazia and South Ossetia (on modalities of security and stability in Abkhazia and

---

5   The French version says "lines", the Russian "line", but this cannot be interpreted in any other way than as a complete withdrawal from Georgia.

South Ossetia).[6] The framework fell short of the original proposal by the EU Presidency, which had called for full respect for the sovereignty and territorial integrity of Georgia and the deployment of an EU or UN peacekeeping force.

The agreed text was presented to EU foreign ministers at an extraordinary European Council meeting on August 13. France also drafted a resolution for the Security Council for approval at a meeting on August 19, in which the Security Council discussed ways to ensure implementation by all parties of the six-point ceasefire agreement. By then, Georgia claimed that it was already fully complying with the ceasefire agreement, but Russia was continuing its occupation. Russia, for its part, claimed it was meeting its obligations under the six-point agreement but was unable to withdraw its troops until Georgia met its obligations, including the return of Georgian troops to their places of permanent deployment.

A draft resolution calling for compliance with the agreement was circulated by France and received the support of a majority of Security Council members. However, Russia objected to the singling out of specific elements of the six-point plan (the call for Russia to withdraw its troops), so no action was taken on the draft.

Russia did not withdraw its troops as agreed, even advancing further into the Akhalgori valley after the agreement had been concluded, thereby establishing control of all the territories of Abkhazia and the former South Ossetian autonomous *oblast*. On August 26, Russia recognized the

---

6  The texts can be compared at https://peacemaker.un.org/sites/peacemaker.un.org/files/GE_080812_Protocol%20d%27accord_0.pdf. There is also an EU translation of the principles at: https://www.eumm.eu/data/file_db/factsheets/.PRES-08-236_EN%20(1).pdf. The agreement also mentions additional security measures to be taken by the Russian peacekeeping forces until the establishment of international mechanisms, an aspect overplayed after the deployment of the European Union Monitoring Mission and Russia's dissolution of its peacekeeping forces.

independence of Abkhazia and South Ossetia, in response to an appeal, according to the Russian narrative, from the South Ossetian and Abkhazian people. Russian troops have been stationed in the regions ever since, the Russian narrative again describing this as in accordance with the wishes and at the invitation of the two states. "Bilateral agreements" have been concluded on the integration and harmonization of the legal, economic, social, security and defense sectors.

In mid-June 2009, a resolution on the extension of the UNOMIG mandate was vetoed by Russia. In the Security Council, Russia argued that UNOMIG's mandate had ceased to exist, owing to Georgian aggression against South Ossetia in August 2008. Russia could not support a mandate aimed at reaffirming the territorial integrity of Georgia, thereby denying the existence of Abkhazia as a state.

The OSCE mission in the Tskhinvali region was also quickly wrapped up because of Russian resistance. Once the EU-brokered six-point plan had been agreed, it was the EU Monitoring Mission (EUMM) and not the OSCE that was tasked with monitoring its implementation. As in the case of UNOMIG, the OSCE shutdown in Georgia was related to lack of agreement on the mandate and work procedures in the country after the war. Russia was not ready to accept that the OSCE office in Tskhinvali should report to the office in Tbilisi, preferring instead direct reporting to Vienna—something that Georgia rejected. Russia also insisted that the mandate of the mission in Tskhinvali was no longer valid since South Ossetia was now also, according to Russia, an independent state. As a result, no agreement could be reached and the OSCE missions in Tbilisi and Tskhinvali fell apart. After months of intensive but fruitless negotiations on extending its mandate, the OSCE mission closed in late 2008.

## Conflict Resolution Mechanisms After the 2008 War

The EUMM, which was tasked with monitoring implementation of the EU-mediated six-point agreement, was deployed in September 2008. The mission's mandate was to provide civilian monitoring of the parties' actions, including their compliance with the six-point agreement and subsequent implementation measures throughout Georgia. In addition, the EUMM was to work in close coordination with partners, in particular the UN and the OSCE, consistent with other EU activity, in order to contribute to stabilization, normalization and confidence building, and thus to long-term stability throughout Georgia, reducing the risk of a resumption of hostilities.

Since the EUMM's deployment, the mission has patroled the areas adjacent to the Administrative Boundary Lines (ABLs) shared with Abkhazia and the Tskhinvali region. Despite its possession of a valid mandate throughout all of Georgia, the de facto authorities in Sukhumi and Tskhinvali — with Russia's backing — have denied the mission access to the territories outside Tbilisi's control. Moreover, Russia's border guards, part of the Federal Security Service (FSB), patrol what in the Russian narrative are called the "state borders".

On October 15, 2008, the Geneva International Discussions (GIDs) were launched to address the security and humanitarian consequences of the August war, co-chaired by representatives of the OSCE, the EU and the UN. A format was agreed after initial negotiations that includes participants from Georgia, Russia and the US, as well as members of both the exiled Georgian administrations from Abkhazia and the Tskhinvali Region/South Ossetia, and the two regions' Russian-backed authorities, the latter in a personal capacity. Sessions are held in two working groups: one discusses peace and security matters, the other humanitarian concerns.

The GIDs continue to be the key platform for all sides to discuss security-related issues and the humanitarian needs of the conflict-affected population. Early on, the sides also managed to agree on proposals for a joint incident prevention and response mechanism (IPRM), aimed at ensuring a timely and adequate response to the security situation, with a particular focus on incident prevention and response.

The GIDs have been marked by disagreements around the return of refugees and IDPs (mostly ethnic Georgians), language (including in schools in predominantly ethnic Georgian areas of Abkhazia), freedom of movement, missing people and cultural heritage, among other things. Over the years, discussions have often deadlocked, but the GIDs' format has managed to survive.

A number of Georgian initiatives have also been taken to reach out to the inhabitants of the regions. The most recent was in 2018, when the Georgian government launched a "new peace policy" with a set of legislative initiatives aimed at enhancing people-to-people exchanges between residents of Abkhazia and South Ossetia, and the rest of Georgia. One initiative, "Step to a better future", has three objectives: (a) facilitating trade across the dividing lines; (b) enhancing educational opportunities in Georgia and abroad; and (c) simplifying access to Georgia's EU integration benefits such as visa waivers, free trade, and so on. An internationally financed "Peace fund for a better future" mechanism has also been set up, which has thus far provided funding for around 40 projects aimed at promoting trade and economic relations among the conflict-divided communities.

Perhaps the most important developments since the six-point agreement in 2008 are the two decisions by the

European Court of Human Rights (ECHR) in 2021. In the first decision, on January 21, in a case filed by Georgia against Russia shortly after the war, the Court recognized the continuing occupation of Georgian territories by the Russian Federation, as well as large-scale violations of the rights of Georgian citizens (the right to life, prohibition of torture, the right to liberty, the right to freedom of movement, property rights and the right to privacy). By explicitly stating that "the strong Russian presence and the South Ossetian and Abkhazian authorities' dependency on the Russian Federation indicates that there has been continued 'effective control' over South Ossetia and Abkhazia", the ECHR asserted the occupation of both South Ossetia and Abkhazia, thereby eliminating any meaningful legal prospect of recognition of their independence, and paving the way for individual lawsuits by hundreds of Georgian citizens against Russia.[7]

In its second decision, on October 21, the ECHR ruled "inadmissible" two applications from Russian citizens living in South Ossetia at the time of the August war against the state of Georgia, alleging human rights violations during the war. With this judgment, the Court dismissed one of Russia's long-standing arguments that atrocities committed by the Georgian side justified its intervention in and subsequent recognition of the occupied territories.

## Conclusions

For the past three decades, Russia has instrumentalized tensions in Georgia and engaged in antagonistic behaviour to further its own geopolitical agenda — in essence to prevent Georgia's escape from Russia's sphere of influence and,

---

[7] European Court of Human Rights, "Case of Georgia vs. Russia", available at http://hudoc.echr.coe.int/eng?i=001-207757.

following Georgia's Rose revolution, obstruct Georgia's turn to the West. Russia has sought to stop Georgia making its own security policy choices, such as joining NATO and the EU, and to dilute the success of its pro-Western, pro-democracy efforts, which could have an impact beyond its borders and threatened the Russian leadership's grip on power.

The international response to Georgia's conflicts was inadequate from the start. While the international community was willing to support Moscow-brokered/dictated ceasefires through its OSCE and UN engagement, the roles of the OSCE and the UN were complicated by the fact that Russia—a permanent member of the UN Security Council and a member of the consensus-driven OSCE—was a party to the conflict. Russia's influence and leverage in the breakaway regions were amplified by the various monitoring and peacekeeping arrangements put in place at the end of the conflicts. Furthermore, this influence and leverage were not only tolerated but blessed by the international community in breach of the key principles of effective conflict resolution—neutrality and the need to command the trust of both conflict parties. The international community left Georgia's fate in Russia's hands, in stark contrast to the engagement in the Balkan conflicts of the same period. Not only Georgia, but European peace and security continue to pay a heavy price for this failure.

In the run-up to the 2008 war, Russia encouraged the perception that the conflicts in Abkhazia and the Tskhinvali region were primarily between the secessionist regions and Tbilisi. While this was a genuine aspect of the conflict, Russia's critical role in supporting the breakaway regions politically, economically and militarily, in undermining Georgian efforts at confidence building, and in the escalation leading up to the 2008 war have been either consistently downplayed or ignored. The fact that Russia acted as a mediator while also an active and destructive party to the conflicts, with its own interests, is another factor that has been neglected over the years, and many countries have partly or fully bought into the Russian narrative.

The unwillingness to highlight Russia's role in the conflicts continued after the 2008 war, despite the hard and well-documented evidence of Moscow's aggressive behavior in and around Georgia's breakaway regions. This included Russia's refusal to honor its commitment to withdraw its military forces from Gudauta in Abkhazia; its deployment of heavy equipment to Abkhazia, while also deploying railway troops to the region in the spring of 2008; and the personnel and equipment it transported to the vicinity around the Roki tunnel, connecting North Ossetia and the Tskhinvali region, in the summer of 2008. The 2008 Kavkaz exercise not only influenced an increasingly nervous government in Tbilisi, but also pre-positioned troops and equipment for the military invasion that followed. Russia justified its involvement partly in terms of preventing a Georgian "genocide" in South Ossetia, and as part of its peacekeeping mission in the region, but none of these justifications have withstood international scrutiny. Medvedev later implicitly admitted that preventing Georgia from joining NATO had been an important consideration.[8]

Russia's use of military force in 2008 further enhanced the country's territorial and military presence in the region at the expense of Georgia's territorial integrity. After concluding agreements with the de facto governments in Abkhazia and South Ossetia, Russia increased its military deployment to bases in both territories and is in fact occupying both regions.

---

8 "Russia says Georgia war stopped NATO expansion", *Reuters*, 21 November 2011, https://www.reuters.com/article/idINIndia-60645720111121.

The weak response of Georgia's partners to Russian actions and involvement in the 2008 war, and Russia's subsequent non-fulfillment of the six-point plan, as well as its absurd recognition of the regions as "independent", at little or no political, economic or other cost, has continued to undermine not only Georgia's territorial integrity, but also European peace and security.

Russia perpetuates the conflicts in Georgia in order to pursue its own geopolitical interests — to secure its influence in the post-Soviet space, to prevent Georgia from moving closer to NATO, and to maintain a military foothold in the country. The final chapter on conflict resolution in Georgia has yet to be written. Its ending will depend not only on decisions taken in Tbilisi and Moscow, but also on what Brussels and Washington decide to do or not to do. It will depend on the conclusions that have been drawn from the inaction and weak response to Russia's war on Georgia in 2008, and since then to Russia's continued policy of aggression in Ukraine and elsewhere.

## Recommendations

**Call a spade a spade.** It is time for an unvarnished call-out of Russia's role in perpetuating the conflicts, consistently and tirelessly in all debates and dialogues no matter the forum, laying bare the fake Russian narrative and Russia's occupation. Better late than never.

**A holistic containment policy.** It is also time that Russia paid a perceptible price for its destructive role, its systematic undermining of the European security order and its continuing breach of agreements and agreed international principles. After years of Russia testing, pushing and overstepping red lines, Georgia being unfortunately only a part of a broader pattern, it is time to step up the defense of the rules-based international order against Russia's deliberate and increasingly flagrant attempts to undermine it. Statements are not enough. The West should take consistent actions in this regard, both in Georgia and elsewhere, even if politically and economically costly.

**End sanction inaction.** Russia is a master at playing for time, wearing down international attention and resistance, creating new "realities on the ground" and repeating its propaganda so many times that it is eventually confused with the truth. The West needs to adapt to these strategies through endurance. In addition, instead of sanctioning only new destructive action, the West should sanction continuing lack of fulfillment of agreed actions; and, after every three or six months of continued inaction, increase the pressure and sanctions.

**Support Georgia's fragile democracy.** Georgia's democracy remains fragile and collusion between illiberal external forces (Russia) and local authoritarian forces risks undermining liberal democratic values. The West has many reasons to assist Georgians to defend themselves by, for instance, promoting economic development, anti-corruption measures, internal political competition and an independent judiciary. It could also further strengthen its engagement with civil society and support for human rights, including minority rights

**Increase the international presence in Georgia.** An increased NATO presence in Georgia would send a particularly strong signal. One example might be a NATO "Center of Excellence" or something similar.

**Maintain the EUMM.** Despite the many limitations on the EUMM's ability to carry out its mission from the outset, it still plays an important role and signals that Russia's failure to comply with the six-point agreement is still a concern. The opposite—disengagement—would send a signal that the EU has either rewarded or given up on changing Russian behavior. EU member states should continue and, if possible, increase their support to the mission.

**Put Georgia back on the international agenda.** In today's increasingly chaotic world, the attention span for each new crisis is short. Nonetheless, Georgia and its unresolved conflicts deserve renewed attention, not least because Georgia's successes — or failures — are not just a Georgian concern but part of a wider (European) peace and security agenda. What we sow in Georgia we will reap elsewhere, but what we fail to sow in Georgia we will also reap elsewhere. Among other things, the EU, the US and like-minded states should work together to increase support for multilateral initiatives related to Georgia's territorial integrity and conduct outreach in support of the non-recognition policy.

**Support Georgia's ability to defend its sovereignty against future external aggression.** It is difficult to conceive how a consolidated democracy can exist without a strong security apparatus capable of responding to the challenges that the country faces. Georgia's defense and security cooperation with the US is especially crucial in this regard. The Memorandum of Understanding on the Georgia Defense and Deterrence Enhancement Initiative recently signed by the countries' defence ministers is a good start. The memorandum aims to replace the Georgia Defense Readiness Program, which concluded at the end of 2021, including the key priorities of strengthening Georgia's capacities for effective deterrence, fostering interoperability with NATO and modernizing Georgia's defense forces. Overall capability to prevent and resilience to respond to hybrid threats should also be increased. This should include additional measures in sensitive and potentially vulnerable parts of Georgia, and in areas with large ethnic minority populations.

**Support Georgia's reconciliation efforts with the regions.** While an end to Russian occupation and support for the secessionist regions are key to restoring Georgia's territorial integrity, there are undoubtedly also local, historical and ethnic aspects to the conflicts. The Georgian government's efforts to reach out to local populations in its new peace initiative should be supported.

**Find ways to break the isolation of people in the separatist regions.** While a local elite might benefit from the current situation, ordinary people in the regions are suffering. The Russian barbed wire along the conflict lines serves (like the Berlin wall seven decades ago) to ensure they are left solidly Russian and subject to Russian narratives. In particular, contacts and travel across the conflict lines should be encouraged, and state services in Georgia, such as health care, facilitated for the inhabitants of the regions.

*Diana Janse is Senior Fellow at the Stockholm Free World Forum. From 2010 to 2014, Janse served as Sweden's ambassador to Georgia. Since 2022, she is State Secretary to Sweden's Minister for International Development Cooperation and Foreign Trade Johan Forssell.*

# Shifting Geopolitical Realities in the South Caucasus

*Stefan Meister*

DOI: https://doi.org/10.24216/9783838216881_006

## Executive Summary

*Azerbaijan's victory in the Second Karabakh War, and its regaining of territory around and partly from the disputed region is not the end, but a new stage of the conflict between Azerbaijan and Armenia. A peace agreement is still far away. Prospects for new connections and trade routes are being challenged by the fragile security situation on the ground, the concerns of several regional states and other unresolved questions. With its "peacekeeping forces", Russian now has troops on the ground in all three states of the South Caucasus. Turkey is increasingly challenging Moscow in the latter's perceived sphere of influence. The geopolitical shift in the region has weakened the European Union's and United States' role in the region and the OSCE Minsk Group as the key multilateral negotiation format. The lack of action by the EU as a mediator or security player in the region has made it easier for other actors to change the rules of the game in the region and weakened democratic progress and reform in the South Caucasus. The formal negotiations aimed at a peaceful political solution have not been able to resolve the conflict in the past 25 years. Military means and authoritarian conflict management might create new geopolitical facts, but will not be able to reconcile the conflict parties. The need for re-engagement and a bigger role for the EU in the region has increased, but without the political will among member states to really strengthen its role in the neighbourhood, nothing will happen. All this plays into the hands of the national elites that gain from the conflict and enemy paradigm. The same is true of external players such as Russia and Turkey, which understand this conflict first and foremost as a part of their power politics.*

## Introduction

The Second Karabakh War of September 27 to November 10, 2020 led to significant death and suffering, and involved serious violations of international humanitarian law and international human rights law. It changed the geopolitical constellation in the South Caucasus and constitutes an example of the inherent instability of the unresolved protracted conflicts in Eastern Europe. Azerbaijan demonstrated that it could turn its defeat of 1994 into a victory with the military support of Turkey and sophisticated weapons. What nearly 30 years of negotiations in the multilateral OSCE Minsk Group could not achieve, Azerbaijan seemed attained in a 44-day war. The ceasefire agreement between Armenia and Azerbaijan, mediated by Russia outside the agreed OSCE format on November 9 and 10, 2020, has utterly changed the situation of the Karabakh conflict and the countries of the South Caucasus.[1] At the same time, it demonstrates the continued practice of dealing with conflicts militarily, as was the case with the First Karabakh War at the beginning of the 1990s when the Armenian side won, laying the ground for further violence and hate fuelled by both sides.

Armenia lost control of all seven of the territories around Karabakh that it had conquered in the early 1990s, with the exception of the five-kilometer-wide Lachin transit corridor between Karabakh and Armenia. It also lost around one-third of the territory of Karabakh itself, including Shusha/Shushi, a town of strategic and historic importance to both sides. Officially, 1,960 Russian peacekeepers are now securing the

---

1 http://kremlin.ru/events/president/news/64384.

territory not regained by Baku. The agreed "corridor" through Armenia along the border with Iran, connecting Azerbaijan with its exclave of Nakhichevan, has not yet been established because of Armenian resistance and is a matter of tensions. Would it be implemented; Armenia would lose even more sovereignty over its territory.

While the "hot war that caused up to 7,000 casualties on both sides has ceased, the conflict is not over; it has merely entered a new phase. Fundamental issues such as the status and administration of Karabakh are still unresolved. The agreement is already being undermined by renewed friction. Especially for Armenia, this humiliating loss has had grave consequences for its domestic politics, including a legitimization crisis for the political elites. At the same time, with its growing dependency on Russian security guarantees, Armenia's national sovereignty is under even greater challenge. In addition, Azerbaijan finds itself in a new situation of having Russian troops on its territory for the first time since the early 1990s.

The balance of power in the region is shifting further away from the EU and the United States towards Russia and Turkey. While the latter was not an official signatory to the ceasefire agreement, Ankara is playing a significant role in the background as a military and diplomatic supporter of Azerbaijan. Israel, too, through its arms deliveries to Baku, has been important to Azerbaijan's victory, and is pursuing its own interests, related particularly to Iran's influence in the region.

By contrast, those actors that had been working for more than 25 years for a peaceful resolution of the conflict on both sides have been further marginalized. The absence of the OSCE Minsk Group or any Western player or international organization (apart from mention of a supervisory role for the UNHCR) from the ceasefire negotiations has undermined the role of multilateral institutions and peaceful conflict resolution mechanisms. This has made Karabakh a peculiar test case of "illiberal peace" and "authoritarian conflict management" by Russia and Turkey.[2] The 44-day war was also the result of Western disengagement, especially in recent years, handing the conflict over to Moscow. Thus, the West itself has contributed to legitimizing Russia's role as the main security player in the South Caucasus. The signaling of this war, that military superiority can lead to a victory without any multilateral engagement, undermines the credibility of Western countries. This war can in its importance for reshuffling regional order not be underestimated.

## The Background to the Second Karabakh War

The conflict between Armenia and Azerbaijan over Karabakh is the longest-running unresolved post-Soviet conflict, which started in 1988 before the break-up of the Soviet Union. An estimated 25,000 lives were lost in inter-ethnic violence and a bitterly fought war in 1992-1994. More than 700,000 ethnic Azeris and over 400,000 ethnic Armenians were forced to flee their often ancestral homelands.

The conflict differs from other protracted conflicts in Eastern Europe, such as those in Moldova, Georgia, and Ukraine, in several respects. First, it is not only by nature, but also by universal and consensual recognition a manifestly interstate conflict between Armenia and Azerbaijan. Even if Armenia has always promoted the de facto authorities as a conflict party in negotiations, Yerevan itself never recognized Karabakh as an independent state. The disputed region

---

[2] See L. Broers, "Requiem for the unipolar moment in Nagorno Karabakh, in: Current history", *Current History*, vol. 120, no. 828, October 2021, 260.

within the internationally recognized borders of Azerbaijan has no direct border with Armenia. Thus, the conquest of some additional Azerbaijani territories was important in order to connect Karabakh directly with Armenian territory and, from an Armenian perspective, to gain buffer zones for security purposes and as bargaining chips. Second, it has long been one of the most dangerous places in the world and, in some respects, more comparable to the confrontations in Kashmir or on the Korean peninsula than to other protracted conflicts in Eastern Europe, which are currently less tense.[3]

A third important element is that Russia has not played the same role as in other protracted conflicts in Eastern Europe. Moscow did not exclusively back one of the conflict parties, in spite of its official alliance with Yerevan. Instead, it developed good relations with both sides and tried to portray itself, with some success, as an honest broker. The Russian leadership was a key negotiator in the OSCE Minsk Group with its other co-chairs, France and the US. This is true to the extent that Russia worked within this group and not unilaterally outside of it, as was the case before and after Russia became one of the three permanent co-chairs. Nonetheless, it has also supplied both sides with weapons and backed the military escalation which it should prevent.

Finally, the struggle over Karabakh has shaped the identity of both countries since the break-up of the Soviet Union, and become an integral part of their nation-building

---

3   I would question this argument with regard to the Donbas where the contact line is a very dangerous place for people. Because of Russian military support and sometimes build-up, the level of militarization is also very high and dangerous for those living close to the contact line. At the same time, according to the number of BICC, the level of militarization between Armenia and Azerbaijan is still higher. See note 6, below, and T. de Waal, "The Nagorny Karabakh conflict in its fourth decade", CEPS Working Document No. 2, September 2021, 2, https://www.ceps.eu/wp-content/uploads/2021/09/WD2021-02_The-Nagorny-Karabakh-Conflict-in-its-Fourth-Decade.pdf (accessed 31 October 2021).

enterprises (alongside related memories in Armenia of the atrocities committed against ethnic Armenians in the Ottoman empire).[4] As in the 1980s and 1990s, Armenia and Azerbaijan each played a part in the latest escalation. The conflict over Karabakh never froze completely. It has always had the potential to escalate and can be described as a low-intensity conflict. Opportunities for peaceful conflict settlement have not been used by either side in the past 25 year and no proper preparations for peace were made by the countries' leaderships vis-à-vis their respective populations.

The two conflicting countries have become two of the most heavily armed states in the world. According to the Global Militarization Index in 2020, Armenia was second and Azerbaijan 16th on the list of the most militarized countries in the world. In 2019, Armenia invested 4.9 percent of its gross domestic product (GDP) and Azerbaijan 4 percent on military expenditure.[5] Azerbaijan funds an immense defense budget with revenues from oil and gas exports. This has allowed the country to buy modern weaponry from Israel, Turkey, Ukraine, Russia and South Korea.[6] Armenia has bought mainly discounted weapons from Russia in the framework of the Russia-led Collective Security Treaty Organization.

While Yerevan could live with the status quo until 2020, it missed several chances to get a better deal during negotiations on a peace agreement in the 25 years before the recent fighting. The Azerbaijani leadership, by contrast, had been

---

[4] Cf. T. de Waal, *The Black Garden: Armenia and Azerbaijan through peace and war* (New York: New York University Press, 2013).

[5] M. Mutschler and M. Bales, Globaler *Militarisierungsindex 2020*, Bonn International Center for Conflict Studies, 7, https://www.bicc.de/uploads/tx_bicc tools/BICC_GMI_2020_DE.pdf (accessed 31 October 2021).

[6] According to SIPRI, Azerbaijan spent US$24 billion on its military between 2009 and 2018. In the same period, Armenia spent US$4 billion on its military, but was able to purchase weapons from Russia at preferential prices in the context of its membership of the CSTO. https://www.sipri.org/sites/default/files/SI PRI-Milex-data-1949-2019.xlsx

increasingly under the impression that Armenia was plotting new baselines—largely ignored by the international community—by building additional infrastructure as well as through its policy of targeted settlements in the occupied territories.[7] In any case, Azerbaijan failed to secure international support for its cause—especially on the issue of its territorial integrity—from any key states other than Turkey. This put Azerbaijan in a different position from Ukraine, Georgia and Moldova, which have also struggled with non-government-controlled areas within their internationally recognized borders.

The democratic election of Nikol Pashinyan after the 2018 Velvet Revolution brought to power a new Armenian Prime Minister who, unlike his predecessors, such as Serzh Sargsyan and Robert Kocharyan, had no roots in Karabakh. This raised hopes of a window of opportunity to resolve the conflict, but these expectations were soon dashed. Pashinyan initially took a moderate tone and appeared to recognize the need to lead his nation out of isolation in order to democratize it. He soon realized, however, that the domestic political costs of a compromise with Azerbaijan would be too high.

As a result, he switched to hardliner rhetoric and was even considering official "integration" of the contested region into Armenia.[8] After a public dispute over history between Azerbaijan's President Ilham Aliyev and Premier Pashinyan at the 2020 Munich Security Conference, it became clear that the leaders of both nations were far apart from each

---

[7] "Digging out of deadlock in Nagorno Karabakh", Report 255, *International Crisis Group*, 20 December 2019, https://www.crisisgroup.org/europe-central-asia/caucasus/nagorno-karabakh-conflict/255-digging-out-deadlock-nagorno-karabakh (accessed 10 October 2021).

[8] With regard to international law, that means annexation of the disputed territory. See "Pashinyan calls for unification between Armenia and Karabakh", *Eurasianet*, 6 August 2019, https://eurasianet.org/pashinyan-calls-for-unification-between-armenia-and-karabakh

other. This meant that a peaceful resolution of the conflict was as unlikely as ever.[9] Nevertheless, Pashinyan cannot be blame first of all for this escalation and war, he had to deal with the legacy of his predecessors which were neither able to negotiate a peace agreement in a time when Armenia had a better bargaining position nor did they invest in the modernization of the Armenian army sufficiently.

At the same time, Aliyev was rhetorically preparing his country for war. A brief military escalation at the Armenian-Azerbaijani border in July 2020 resulted in the loss of a high-ranking Azerbaijani officer. The timing and preparations for war were carried out in a planned and calculated way. At the same time, one factor that should not be underestimated was the requirement for Aliyev to react to an accelerating nationalist dynamic in his country, one that could easily have spilled into the streets and challenged his legitimacy. As a result, in the shadow of the global COVID-19 pandemic and the 2020 US presidential election campaign, and ahead of winter, he began the 44-day war for Karabakh in September 2020.

## Shifting the Regional Balance of Power

A key outcome of the Second Karabakh War has been a shift in the regional balance of power, as both Russia and Turkey increased their influence in the wider region. Russia's main interests in the South Caucasus are to remain the dominant regional military and security player, and to push or keep other actors, particularly the US, NATO and the EU, out of the region. Having stationed Russian "peacekeeping forces" in Karabakh, Moscow now has troops in all three states of the Southern Caucasus. Even though Turkey also has a foothold

---

9   Munich Security Conference, "An update on Nagorno-Karabakh", https://www.facebook.com/watch/live/?v=480692625931370&ref=external

in the region, Ankara is not able to challenge Moscow's hegemonic position. Russia's war against Ukraine will impact on the situation in the South Caucasus. The outcome of this war will shift on the geopolitical and security situation in the region. At the same time, Russia will have in the foreseeable future sufficient resources, to stay the key security player in the South Caucasus.

Baku may have communicated its planned military action in advance not only to Ankara, but also to Moscow, which was probably informed about the forthcoming escalation by its intelligence services anyway. Nonetheless, the rapid territorial gains by Azerbaijani troops might still have taken Moscow by surprise. The Russian leadership managed to negotiate a ceasefire agreement before Azerbaijan's army regained all of Karabakh. This also allowed Russia to give itself a new role in the disputed region by officially dispatching almost 2,000 peacekeepers, albeit without a formal internationally recognized mandate.

There is apparently a document that defines the legal framework for the peacekeeping operation, but Azerbaijan has not signed it.[10] The mandate for the Russian mission needs to be renewed after five years—a provision that is in Baku's interest, because it provides an opportunity to cancel the agreement. Azerbaijani experts, moreover, allege that the Russian military and non-military contingent has in fact grown to 7,000-8,000 personnel.[11] As Armenian military units withdrew, Moscow de facto replaced Yerevan as the patron of Karabakh. Russian has been introduced as a second

---

10 V. Huseynov, "Azerbaijan increasingly critical of Russia's peacekeeping mission in Karabakh", *Eurasia Daily Monitor*, vol. 18, no. 144, 22 September 2021, https://jamestown.org/program/azerbaijan-increasingly-critical-of-russias-peacekeeping-mission-in-karabakh/ (accessed 2 November 2021).
11 Ibid.

language in the disputed region and has become the only security guarantee for disputed region.[12]

Russia's actions have also marginalized the OSCE Minsk Group, thereby further reducing the already relatively low influence of the US and the EU, via France, in the region (to the extent that France represented EU positions, which was not always the case). Even if the Minsk Group retains the sole official international mandate to negotiate an agreement, the crucial talks are taking place between Russia, Armenia, Azerbaijan and, partly, Turkey. Nevertheless, it could be important to keep the existing infrastructure of the OSCE Minsk group if the situation in the conflict is changing.

The Moscow-brokered ceasefire agreement, which does not make any reference to the existing OSCE formats, did not just make Russia even more important for Armenia as a protective power. Azerbaijan, too, must now come to terms with a Russian presence on its territory for the first time since 1993. While President Aliyev claims that the conflict is over, he still lacks full sovereignty and territorial integrity. Moreover, Moscow has succeeded in keeping Turkey out of the agreement, although there is a monitoring mechanism with some Turkish involvement. At a joint monitoring center with Russia, Turkey has deployed 45 monitors 20 km from the front line, on Azerbaijani territory.[13]

The Russian leadership's wait-and-see approach during the war showed that Moscow has other goals than simply to support its "ally" Armenia, although Armenian territorial integrity definitely remains a red line until now. Until the 2020 war, Moscow had only limited influence over Azerbaijan, which used gas and oil pipelines that circumvented Russian

---

12 De Waal (2021), 8, n. 3.
13 See "Post-war prospects for Nagorno-Karabakh", *International Crisis Group*, Report 264, 9 June 2021, https://d2071andvip0wj.cloudfront.net/264-nagorno-karabakh.pdf (accessed 31 October 2021).

territory for its energy exports through Georgia to Europe. Now, with the Russian troops on Azerbaijani territory key to the negotiations between Armenia and Azerbaijan, Russia has increased its leverage on Baku. But if these forces do not react to Azerbaijani provocations, Baku might try to systematically force Armenia to agree with its demands based on military pressure.

Turkey's support for Azerbaijan shifted the balance in the Karabakh conflict and was key to Baku's military victory. For years, Azerbaijan had been arming itself with state-of-the-art drones and precision weapons to prepare for war.[14] As a NATO member, Turkey helped to improve the capabilities of the Azerbaijani army with training and joint exercises. It also gave Baku a clear military-technological advantage by providing drones, as well as the relevant operating systems and on-site technical support. Multiple sources have confirmed that up to 2,000 Syrian combatants were brought in with Turkish support, boosting the military capacity of the Azerbaijani army.[15] President Recep Erdoğan's unconditional support for Azerbaijan on the international stage gave Baku the feeling that it had a true ally. That was also crucial, for starting this war. While it may have been domestically advantageous for Turkey's president to score points with nationalists by supporting Azerbaijan, it was also important to challenge Russia in its sphere of influence. He thereby

---

14  Between 2014 and 2018, Azerbaijan was the second largest buyer of Israeli weapons, accounting for 17 percent of Israeli exports. "Trends in international arms trade, 2018", *SIPRI factsheet*, March 2019, https://www.sipri.org/sites/default/files/2019-03/fs_1903_at_2018.pdf

15  "Russian FM: 2000 Mideast militants fight in Nagorno-Karabakh", *Associated Press*, 3 November 2020, https://apnews.com/article/2000-mideast-milliants-nagorno-karabakh-1d24df0044dc17f54ce4f45380505cf0; "Deaths of Syrian mercenaries show how Turkey, Russia could get sucked into Nagorno-Karabakh conflict", *Washington Post*, 14 October 2020, https://www.washingtonpost.com/world/middle_east/azerbaijan-armenia-turkey-nagorno-karabakh/2020/10/13/2cdca1e6-08bf-11eb-8719-0df159d14794_story.html

improved his bargaining position vis-à-vis Moscow in other conflicts, such as Syria and Libya.

The Turkish leadership is critical of Moscow's attempt to tip the military balance in its favour in the Black Sea, especially after Russia's illegal annexation of Crimea and its war against Ukraine. Through its indirect intervention in the Karabakh conflict, Turkey has indicated its ambition to become an even more influential power in the South Caucasus, and to regain some of the influence it had in the time of the Ottoman empire. Against the background of declining US interest in the region and the EU's lack of interest in security-related engagement, states such as Georgia and Ukraine increasingly perceive Ankara as an ally to counterbalance Russia in the Black Sea region.

The 2020 Azerbaijani victory strengthens the Baku-Ankara axis, allowing Turkey to continue to pursue its economic and energy policy interests in the Caspian Sea region and Asia. Ankara has upgraded the Turkish Armed Forces' representation in the Azerbaijan Operational Group by adding four generals to the leadership. Furthermore, both armies held military exercises only 300 meters from the Lachin corridor in September 2021.[16] With systematic military pressure on Armenia and latest attacks on Armenian territory, president Aliyev systematically use his military superiority to get a "peace agreement" under his terms and to get a direct connection between Azerbaijan and its exclave Nakhichevan. Additionally, President Aliyev has an interest in safeguarding Azerbaijan (with its largely Shia population) as a secular state, not letting Sunni-Islamist ideology spread or Turkish power to become too dominant in the country. Here contradictory become positions between Ankara and Baku become visible.

---

16  Cf. Huseynov, 2021.

The agreed corridor through Armenia to the Azerbaijani exclave of Nakhichevan is source of potential conflict, with regard both to its use by Turkey and Azerbaijan, and to Azerbaijan's future relations with Iran. In addition, President Aliyev's July 2021 comment on this part of Armenia ("West Zangazur is our historical land") indicates possible Azerbaijani territorial claims to Armenian territory, at least for negotiation purposes. But non reaction by Russia and the international community to Azerbaijani attacks against Armenian territory could fuel more territorial demands from the Azerbaijani side. Located along the border with Iran in Armenia's Syunik province, the connection could become a problem rather than opportunity for trade and transit between Armenia and Iran. Iran is an important economic and energy partner for Armenia, and Armenia sees this partnership as the only way to mitigate, at least partially, its economic and energy dependence on Russia by getting gas from Iran. The creation of such a corridor secured by Russian border guards would further undermine the sovereignty of the Armenian state.

For the Iranian leadership, it is important that Russia has a presence in the region, and that its rival Turkey cannot establish dominance in Azerbaijan. The huge number of ethnic Azeris in northern Iran is also important for Tehran. While Iran has called for the return of the seven territories around Karabakh to Azerbaijan, Tehran welcomes the fact that Karabakh was not fully retaken by Azerbaijani troops, and that Russian forces will be deployed in the disputed territory for at least five years.[17] For Tehran, military cooperation between Azerbaijan and Israel is especially problematic. Iranian companies were not invited by Baku to help rebuild the

---

17 "How Iran sees the Nagorno-Karabakh truce", *Eurasianet*, 13 November 2020, https://eurasianet.org/perspectives-how-iran-views-the-nagorno-karabakh-truce.

reconquered territories, but Israeli companies were offered opportunities to participate in the rebuilding of areas that border Iran.

For several years, Tehran has accused Israel of using Azerbaijani territory for intelligence purposes and for launching military actions against Iran. The Azerbaijani state border service patrols the border with Iran with the help of Israeli-made drones. In reaction, both Azerbaijan (in cooperation with Turkey and Pakistan) and Iran have organized large-scale military exercises on their respective borders.[18]

## Armenia and Azerbaijan: The Limits of the Victory

After Armenia's 2018 Velvet Revolution and a competitive democratic election, there were high hopes in the country that this was the moment for fundamental reforms and integration into the democratic world. Even though the challenges facing Pashinyan were huge, he also failed due to his apparent unwillingness to initiate a fundamental reform process. His manual rule, his populist style and way of dealing with the media alienated the progressive parts of society. Nonetheless, despite Armenia's defeat in the Second Karabakh War, Pashinyan managed to get re-elected in snap elections in June 2021. This was more due to a lack of alternatives and the even lower rating of his challengers, most notably former president Robert Kocharyan (who has close ties with Russia), than to strong support for Pashinyan. But it was also a strong signal of the society, that it wants not return to the corrupt and autocratic leadership of the past but demands reforms and progress from its leadership.

---

18  R. Mammadli, "What is behind the growing Iran-Azerbaijan tension?", *OC Media*, 11 October 2021, https://oc-media.org/features/analysis-what-is-behind-the-growing-iran-azerbaijan-tension/ (accessed 2 November 2021).

After the 2020 war, Armenia had to adjust to the reality that the Western community, despite some rhetorical support, had left the country to fend for itself in and around Karabakh, but also that it could not count on Russia as a protective power. Moscow's wait-and-see approach until the moment before an Armenian defeat, and its pronounced neutrality, were a source of deep frustration for Armenia. Even though the alliance option under the CSTO only applied to the territory of Armenia itself, Moscow's muted response showed Yerevan that this post-Soviet institution is something of a Potemkin organization, by the grace of Moscow, rather than a functional military alliance. That Belarus or Kazakhstan, as CSTO member states, could support Armenia militarily in its war against Azerbaijan was also out of the question, at least as long as there was no Russian leadership.

Russia's military presence extends beyond Karabakh. In Armenia, Moscow operates a military base in Gyumri, the second-largest city in the country, with 3,000 military personnel. Russia is playing a crucial role in securing the transit route between Armenia and the disputed region, as well as with regard to the possible corridor to Nakhichevan for Azerbaijan and Turkey. It has deployed troops close to Armenia's border with Azerbaijan as well as with Turkey at the request of Yerevan. All this contributes to Armenia's further lost sovereignty.

Without Russian support Armenia is not able to protect itself. This gives Russia even greater influence over Armenian domestic politics. It is conceivable that the Kremlin's reluctance to help Yerevan in 2020 was also intended to weaken the position of Prime Minister Pashinyan. He had come to power in 2018 via street protests and democratic elections, something that is a nightmare for the Kremlin in view of the domestic politics of Russia and other Eastern European states, not least Belarus. But more important for the Kremlin seemed to be to get its forces on Azerbaijani soil than to stop the war earlier.

For Armenia, the 2020 ceasefire agreement was tantamount to capitulation—not only undermining its understanding of Armenian sovereignty, but also destabilizing the country as a whole. Pashinyan discredited himself in the eyes of many Armenians by signing the agreement with Aliyev. The wave of refugees from Karabakh and the surrounding provinces, as well as the dead, wounded, missing and returning soldiers, have caused additional burdens on Armenia. According to Armenian sources, more than 300 POWs are still missing. These have not only weakened the country financially. They also have destabilizing effects on society because of the many frustrated and homeless people. According to unofficial statistics, up to 100,000 people live in Karabakh and there are now more than 20,000 permanent refugees from the region in Armenia.[19]

The still unresolved status and administration of Karabakh remain contentious issues that will continue to affect domestic politics in Armenia and Azerbaijan, and to cause lasting instability in the South Caucasus. An open wound persists between Armenians and Azerbaijanis. Armenian politicians have limited room for compromise after the 2020 defeat. National security and sovereignty, as they are understood in Armenia, have become even more pressing issues.

The lack of border demarcation between Armenia and Azerbaijan will further fuel tensions between both countries. Be it border questions, captured soldiers or lethal landmines, security issues have become political bargaining chips and

---

19   Author's interview with an expert on the region, April 2021.

toxic topics in the relations between the two states.[20] Since the 2020 war, it appears unlikely that any of the recent Armenian refugees will ever return to the areas now controlled by Russian forces. Many no longer believe they can rely on Russia's protection. Today, it is even more difficult than before 2020 to envisage Armenians and Azerbaijanis peacefully and cooperatively coexisting.

Whereas before the war Azerbaijan's President Aliyev had offered the "highest possible autonomy existing in the world" for the people living in Karabakh,[21] he has recently announced that there will be no territorial autonomy at all. For the Azerbaijani side, Karabakh "no longer exists as a concept".[22] Baku uses its new position of power to try to put Armenia under further military pressure to resolve open questions in Azerbaijan's interest. This will cause further flight and displacement, and presumably increase the tensions between the neighbors. Armenia has shifted its approach from autonomy of Karabakh Armenians to the demand for human rights guarantees by Baku.

Baku is now engaged in rapid demining efforts in the disputed region and its surroundings, as well as in large infrastructure projects there. With these activities, as well as new housing development and industrial investment by Turkey and Russia, new facts on the ground are emerging. Azerbaijan has already invested US$3 billion in the reconquered regions, almost completely restored the electricity supply to the entire region and announced plans to build smart

---

20 Cf. International Crisis Group (2021).
21 "Azerbaijan president's perspective on Nagorno Karabakh impasse resolution", *Eurasia*, 24 June 2011, https://www.euronews.com/2011/06/24/azerbaijan-president-s-perspective-on-nagorno-karabakh-impasse-resolution.
22 J. Kucera, "Down with Nagorno Karabakh — long live Karabakh", *Eurasianet*, 2 April 2021, https://eurasianet.org/down-with-nagorno-karabakh-long-live-karabakh (accessed 31 October 2021).

villages.²³ It will be costly to rebuild the largely destroyed infrastructure in the seven territories Baku has restored to its full control, where it plans to resettle some of the 700,000 internally displaced persons (IDPs) who had to leave their homeland in the early 1990s.

Among those most affected by these new developments in the past year are civil society and the peace activists in both countries. The pressure on Armenian civil society, especially those who cooperated with Western institutions and participated in reconciliation measures with Azerbaijani partners, increased during the war. The story is similar in Azerbaijan where, in the national frenzy of war and victory, anyone who campaigned for peace was considered a traitor and even persecuted by the state authorities.²⁴

The local forces that had been calling for reconciliation have lost much since 2020. Nationalists and hardliners now dominate the political discourse in both countries. This will weaken general civil society development and makes achieving a lasting peace much less likely. The 2020 military victory boosted the legitimacy of President Aliyev, providing him with more scope to put critics under pressure. Many in the opposition support the patriotic victory paradigm and alternate voices have become rare.²⁵ At the same time, the Azerbaijani victory might make it easier to negotiate a compromise, and the possible rapprochement between Turkey and

---

23   P. Globe, "Karabakh conflict continues through competing construction projects", *Eurasia Daily Monitor*, vol. 18, no. 162, 26 October 2021, https://jamestown.org/program/karabakh-conflict-continues-through-competing-construction-projects/ (accessed 3 November 2021).
24   "Azerbaijani Security Services 'threatened to kill' activist and family", *OC Media*, 16 November 2020, https://oc-media.org/azerbaijani-security-services-threatened-to-kill-activist-and-family/
25   B. Samadov, "To stand for peace in spite of everything", *OC Media*, 2 October 2020, https://oc-media.org/opinions/opinion-to-stand-for-peace-in-spite-of-everything/.

Armenia could support this process. But it will come at the costs of Armenia.

## The Decline of Western Influence

For the EU and the US, the Second Karabakh War and ceasefire agreement of late 2020 marked a spectacular failure of their various efforts to contribute to stabilization, confidence building and conflict resolution. The OSCE Minsk Group format had been the main multilateral framework for negotiations since the First Karabakh War in 1992. Through the Group's co-chairs, France, Russia and the US, two major Western powers were involved in conflict mediation.

Neither the EU nor the US played any role in the negotiations on the ceasefire between Armenia and Azerbaijan in 2020. Russia's blatant bypassing of the OSCE Minsk Group format and High-Level Planning Group, which had been preparing for a multinational OSCE peacekeeping force to Karabakh since 1994, fits into the larger context of growing tensions between Moscow and the West in recent years. The war in Ukraine has made it even more difficult, to cooperate on the conflict. As a result of their inaction, the EU and the US have been effectively pushed out of the conflict resolution process, weakening the role of the OSCE. Although there was a meeting of the three co-chairs at a side event of the 76th UN General Assembly in New York in September 2021, neither Washington nor Paris has an impact on the dynamics and mediation of the conflict. Instead, Russia was able to create major new facts on the ground with its unilateral deployment of peacekeeping forces to Karabakh.[26]

---

26 "Statement by the Co-Chairs of the OSCE Minsk Group," *OSCE*, 24 September 2021, https://www.osce.org/minsk-group/498948 (accessed 31 October 2021).

While the Minsk Group has lost both functionality and legitimacy, the conflict parties may still have an interest in using the format for peace negotiations. Armenia, in particular, with its weakened bargaining position, has an interest in bringing additional actors into the settlement process, although obviously not Turkey, a Minsk Group member, whose participation Azerbaijan would insist on in the case of a change to the format. It is also up to Moscow and, to some extent, Baku to decide on the role of the OSCE in future negotiations—and on the ground, where the Personal Representative of the Chairperson-in-Office has until now played a limited role. The appointment of a new co-chair by the US might bring some new life into the format, although the Russian-US tensions about the war in Ukraine will undermine any kind of rapprochement. In the meantime, the process of border demarcation and delimitation between Armenia and Azerbaijan, based on Soviet-era maps, and without specifying the status of Karabakh, has begun within the trilateral format with Moscow.[27]

For Azerbaijan, it has always been problematic that the three countries with the world's largest Armenian diasporas constitute the three co-chairs of the Minsk Group. France and the US had grown frustrated with the conflict parties over the years and reduced their engagement with the Minsk Group format, which resulted in Russia increasingly dominating the negotiations. When French President Emmanuel Macron sided with Armenia during the 2020 war, that made it even

---

27 V. Huseynov, "'Zangezur Corridor' closer to realization as Armenia readies to normalize relations with Turkey and Azerbaijan", *Eurasia Daily Monitor*, vol. 18, no. 158, 19 October 2021, https://jamestown.org/program/zangazur-corridor-closer-to-realization-as-armenia-readies-to-normalize-relations-with-turkey-and-azerbaijan/ (accessed 3 November 2021).

more difficult for Baku to accept Paris as an honest conflict broker.[28]

The fact that Russia negotiated the ceasefire agreement outside the Minsk Group format has created a new reality. The West is no longer part of the conflict mediation and resolution process. For the Russian leadership, it has been easier to reach partial accord with Ankara than with Washington and Paris. There were some hopes, that the newly established facilitation format by the EU under Charles Michel would create a new opportunity for EU engagement aiming on practical steps like the release of Armenian POWs by Azerbaijan, progress in border limitations and the negotiation of a peace agreement. But since the EU is not using its leverage on the two conflicting sides, it has very limited impact on enforcing any kind of agreement. Instead of creating an alternative negotiation format, the EU has become rather a neutral facilitator without much impact on dynamics on the ground.

Western inaction before and during the 2020 war has not only discredited democracy and the EU in the whole region, but also led to a loss of credibility for the stakeholders in government, parliament and civil society who campaigned for a European and democratic Armenia. This has harmed the EU's neighborhood policy, of which Armenia was once considered a role model, as it is both a member of the Eurasian Economic Union and a signatory of a Comprehensive and Enhanced Partnership Agreement with the EU. Especially the opposition is using the slogan democracy or security to undermine the government of Nikol Pashinyan and discredit the Velvet revolution.

---

28 "Macron says France ready to help build lasting solution to Nagorno-Karabakh conflict", *Radio Free Europe/Radio Liberty*, 13 November 2020, https://www.rferl.org/a/macron-france-ready-lasting-solution-karabakh-conflict/30946318.html (accessed 31 October 2021).

That the Karabakh conflict was underestimated by the EU sends multiple geopolitical messages and has an impact beyond the region. In the South Caucasus, Turkey's arrival and Iran's engagement, which is expected to grow in the light of Israeli and Turkish activities, are causing further disintegration of the post-Soviet space. Russia's role in reaching a ceasefire agreement and its deployment of peacekeeping forces demonstrated that it is still the key security player in the South Caucasus, but it is increasingly being challenged by countries such as Turkey, Iran and China — especially in the economic and transport sectors. The Kremlin's policy of taking advantage of conflicts rather than resolving them, however, can only work as long as Russia has sufficient resources to back up that policy with military force. Therefore, the outcome of the war in Ukraine will play an important role for the security situation in the South Caucasus.

Turkey is seeking direct access to the Caspian Sea and is getting closer to its goal of becoming a hub for energy resources from the Caspian Sea to Europe. In the light of the decoupling from Russian oil and gas, the EU will have an increasing interest in Azerbaijani hydrocarbons and a possible transcaspian link to buy gas from Central Asia. In this context Turkey will be even more important as a transit route for oil and gas to Europe. Turkey's military and economic cooperation with Azerbaijan have improved Ankara's position in its negotiations with Moscow. Countries such as Georgia and Ukraine will keep a close eye on players that can balance Russia's influence in the region in the future. Turkey supplies drones to Ukraine and is discussed in the region as a possible partner in confronting Russia if the US withdraws further from the region and the EU remains unwilling to engage more on security issues.[29] But, the economic crisis in Turkey ahead of the 2023 elections and its ongoing demand for Russian resources shows the limits of Ankara's approach.

Russia, Turkey, and Iran have a common interest in building transit routes through the South Caucasus. This opens up certain opportunities for rapprochement between Armenia and Turkey, and the possibility of open borders between both countries. But for Turkey it will depend on the reaction of Baku, if it finalizes the border opening negotiations. Georgia is playing a mediating role in the negotiations between both countries. Nonetheless, a precondition for improvement in relations between Ankara and Yerevan remains normalization of relations between Armenia and Azerbaijan. While there is potential for increased trade and connectivity, and expectations are high following the war, without a real peace agreement there are also many remaining obstacles.[30]

Ankara, Tehran and Moscow have proposed a 3+3 format between the three South Caucasian states, Turkey, Iran and Russia.[31] This would cement the new geopolitical reality without the EU or the US. It would also create a platform for the negotiation of new large-scale infrastructure projects. Tbilisi is currently opposed to such an initiative, however, and will not participate in any such regional format with Moscow

---

29 "Ukraine uses Turkish armed drone in Donbas for 1st time", *Hürriyet Daily News*, 27 October 2021, https://www.hurriyetdailynews.com/ukraine-uses-tu rkish-armed-drone-in-donbas-for-1st-time-168922 (accessed 31 October 2021).
30 T. de Waal, "In the South Caucasus, Can new trade routes help overcome a history of conflict?", *Carnegie Europe*, 8 November 2021, https://carnegieeurope .eu/2021/11/08/in-south-caucasus-can-new-trade-routes-help-overcome-hist ory-of-conflict-pub-85729.
31 E. Teslova, "Russia suggests 3+3 format with Turkey, Iran, Azerbaijan, Armenia, Georgia in the Caucasus", *Anadolu Agency*, 6 October 2021, https://www. aa.com.tr/en/politics/russia-suggests-3-3-format-with-turkey-iran-azerbaijan -armenia-georgia-in-caucasus/2384679 (accessed 3 November 2021).

until Russian troops leave Abkhazia and South Ossetia.[32] For Tbilisi, new East-West transit routes through Azerbaijan and Armenia would undermine Georgia's role as the key transit country. It would also be affected by possible new South-North transit routes connecting Russia, and Iran via Azerbaijan. However, Georgia's democratic backsliding in the context of its 2018 presidential elections, 2020 parliamentary elections and 2021 local elections has led to Tbilisi's estrangement from the EU. Against this background, the three large regional powers will make a further push for a 3+3 format.

The problem of the EU's engagement in the South Caucasus and elsewhere is that it is not a relevant geopolitical player. Its resulting failure to act and engage has consequences for the stability and development of its neighbors, which will be increasingly influenced by other actors. In a multipolar world, this leads to instability. The withdraw of the US from several regions and its towards China and the Asia Pacific region is creating a geopolitical vacuum on the EU's southern and eastern borders, in which players such as Russia, Turkey, Saudi Arabia and Iran will be competing for influence. The return of the US to Europe in the light of Russia's war in Ukraine does not mean, that Washington will also engage in other regions of conflict at Europes margins. Even if the EU remains a mere onlooker, it will face direct consequences from the conflicts, war, displacement, migration and instability that will plague nearby weak states.

The EU is losing credibility among the neighborhood's civil societies and democratic stakeholders in government and parliament. Its failure to act on security challenges has

---

32 V. Kaleki, "Iran and the 3+3 regional cooperation format in the South Caucasus: Strengths and weaknesses", *Eurasia Daily Monitor*, vol. 18, no. 96, 16 June 2021, https://jamestown.org/program/iran-and-the-33-regional-cooperation-format-in-the-south-caucasus-strengths-and-weaknesses/ (accessed 3 November 2021).

substantially weakened democracy and the rule of law on its borders, where the "right of the mighty" has prevailed over the "might of right". Lasting peace can, however, only be achieved through trust-building, compromise and reconciliation, and not through military victories—a lesson learned from the First Karabakh War and, as it turned out, its uncertain results.

## Recommendations

1. The EU needs to engage more in conflict management, monitoring and peacekeeping in all of the protracted conflicts in Eastern Europe. In addition to its important role as a key donor and promoter of dialogue, it needs to become a relevant actor in establishing and securing lasting peace in the South Caucasus through stronger involvement in negotiations in multilateral formats. It needs to be more invested in the various negotiation platforms, including those of the OSCE, and more willing to deploy peacekeepers and monitoring missions to safeguard ceasefires. It might make sense to promote the UN's role in peacekeeping in the region, but it should be expected that Russia will block any decision in its role as a permanent member of the UN Security Council.

2. Bringing the EU or certain nonpartisan states into the conflict mediation and resolution process could be an instrument for reanimating the OSCE Minsk Group. France could be replaced by the EU through its Special Representative. In the current constellation, with France, Russia and the US as co-chairs, the group will face difficulties in regaining its past relevance. Upgrading the mandate of the EU's Special Representative could be an important step towards increasing the profile of the EU in the conflict. It would also demand more backing from the EU member states.

3. The EU needs to start an honest discussion on how to deal with Russia in conflicts, in the post-Soviet space, including in the context of Karabakh; and on how to better help the people on the ground. With Russia's war in Ukraine it is not anymore acceptable, that Russia is using the undermining the security of sovereign. Inaction will push Karabakh and Armenia deeper into Russia's embrace and accepts Baku's approach, that military solution of a conflict is an option without creating lasting peace and stability. There is a need for clearer rules for dealing with Russia regarding these conflicts, and for more ownership of the settlement process by multilateral institutions and the EU itself — for instance, by providing international peacekeeping troops and ensuring comprehensive monitoring of borders.

4. The parties to the Karabakh conflict have an interest in a greater role for international organizations in the conflict. The internationalization of the Karabakh conflict is a precondition for a peaceful solution. The UN should discuss how to position itself on non-UN-mandated peacekeeping forces.

5. An honest assessment is required of what went wrong in past conflict mediation and dialogue projects. The EU and international organizations should refocus their attention on such conflict-related challenges as refugees, IDPs, war crimes, human rights violations and housing issues. Material humanitarian support is not enough, for instance, to help IDPs. Work is also needed with the people on the ground on their traumas, their individual fates and their tragic experiences, and to change the narratives about the other side and the conflict. Of course, this is also a major task for the governments and societies of both countries.

6. It is up to the political elites and civil societies of Armenia and Azerbaijan to start a genuine reconciliation process and end the rhetoric of hate and antagonism. Since the

end of the 1980s, the populations of both countries have had practically no contact. Better conditions for dialogue initiatives and confidence building might create more acceptance for the negotiation of a lasting peace agreement. But first a functioning ceasefire as to be created.

7. Civil society and international organizations should put more effort into challenging the current adversarial discourses and situating the conflict in the context of human rights protection and non-discrimination policies. All the conflict parties should actively work on a deconstruction of "threats" in their societies, and on sending respectful messages to the other parties to the conflict, as well as on confidence building and the development of a vision for a common future.[33] This is paramount in overcoming the prevailing narratives of hate and paradigms of humiliation. More support for democratic development, and respect for human rights and the rule of law, in both Azerbaijan and Armenia through the Eastern Partnership could have positive effects on interstate relations between the two countries.

*Dr. Stefan Meister is Head of the International Order and Democracy Program at the German Council on Foreign Relations in Berlin.*

---

33  Cf. L. Alieva, "War in the Caucasus—Karabagh conflict: Why war?", *International Institute for Peace*, 13 October 2020, https://www.iipvienna.com/new-blog/2020/10/13/karabagh-conflict-why-war (accessed 31 October 2021).

# Part II.

# Protracted Conflicts, European Security and International Law

# Conflict-Solving Mechanisms and Negotiation Formats for Post-Soviet Protracted Conflicts
## A Comparative Perspective

*Stefan Wolff*

DOI: https://doi.org/10.24216/9783838216881_007

## Executive Summary

*The OSCE area has been plagued by protracted conflicts for several decades. These are long-lasting, identity-based conflicts that involve contestations over territory. They are state-based, but often internationalized, thus also affecting relations between OSCE participating States. As such, they are a legitimate concern for the Organization whose mandate is focused on comprehensive and cooperative security.*

*Protracted conflicts in the OSCE area include, among others, the conflicts in Northern Ireland and Cyprus, which date back to the Cold War, the ones in Kosovo and the Republika Srpska in Bosnia and Herzegovina, both of which had their origins in the prolonged disintegration of Yugoslavia, and the conflict over Crimea between Ukraine and Russia.*

*Of particular interest for this report, because they involve the OSCE in a conflict-management role, are the conflicts on the territory of the former Soviet Union occasionally but erroneously described as "frozen". These include the conflicts over Transnistria in Moldova, over Abkhazia and South Ossetia in Georgia, and the one between Armenia and Azerbaijan over Nagorno-Karabakh. The latest additions to this list are the conflicts over the so-called "Donetsk*

People's Republic" and "Lugansk People's Republic" (Russ. abbr.: DNR, LNR) in the Donbas area of Ukraine.[1]

For the most part, these conflicts have been managed with varying degrees of success. Several of them have reached a more or less stable equilibrium (Transnistria, Abkhazia, South Ossetia, Crimea), while others remain in a low-intensity state (Donbas). Events in and around Nagorno-Karabakh in the autumn of 2020, meanwhile, serve as a reminder that the label "frozen" is misleading for these conflicts, as there is always a danger of a resurgence of violence, something also evidenced in relation to Abkhazia and South Ossetia in the context of the Russo-Georgian war of 2008.

The protracted conflicts in the post-Soviet space have a geopolitical dimension. The general deterioration of relations between east and west has accelerated since the unilateral declaration of independence by Kosovo and the Russo-Georgian war of 2008 and, in an even more pronounced way, since the beginning of the crisis in Ukraine in late 2013. For over a decade, this has been the context in which the management of these conflicts has not only failed to make any substantial progress towards sustainable negotiated solutions, but has also seen a significant deterioration of security and stability on the ground.

In addition, renewed geopolitical rivalry has turned the states affected by protracted conflicts into targets of competitive influence-seeking, with detrimental effects for the affected populations, states, and societies, and contributing to a lack of political stability and economic development, increasing fragility of core state institutions, and deteriorating human rights conditions.

---

1   Arguably, other conflicts could be added to this list: the conflict over South Tyrol between Italy and Austria from 1946 to 1969 (formally declared resolved in 1993), the conflicts in the Basque country and Catalonia in Spain, and the conflict over Corsica in France. Apart from South Tyrol, the Northern Ireland conflict is the only case of a protracted conflict in the OSCE area that could be considered resolved, albeit with some question marks concerning the impact of the UK's exit from the European Union.

*As they have become new arenas in which geopolitical rivalries are played out, the negotiation formats in the protracted conflicts in Moldova, Ukraine, Georgia, and Azerbaijan, which are the focus of the following analysis, have also been negatively affected by these developments. At the same time, negotiated settlements are the stated preferred outcome for the overwhelming majority of participating States, although they have either not yet materialized (Transnistria, Abkhazia, South Ossetia, Nagorno-Karabakh) or not yet been implemented (the Minsk Accords in Donbas).*

*This is not the fault of the existing negotiation formats per se, but rather that of the participants themselves, whose unwillingness to make concessions and compromises represents the main stumbling block in reaching sustainable negotiated settlements. Over the years and decades, the immediate conflict parties have often sought unrealistic maximal gains at the negotiation table, gains that they could not achieve on the battlefield, and their external backers have lacked the leverage (or the willingness to use it) to incentivize or pressure them to moderate their demands.*

*Although the existing negotiation formats have failed to reach their ultimate objective of reaching sustainable settlements, they have been important in stabilizing volatile situations, providing humanitarian relief, and addressing issues that fall short of political settlement questions (such as economic connectivity, freedom of movement, and environmental management). These smaller, but nonetheless important successes have, to a significant degree, been due to OSCE efforts, especially those focused on mediation and confidence building.*

*Acknowledging the ongoing complexity of the protracted conflicts in the OSCE area and analyzing conflict management successes and failures to date, this report makes seven recommendations to the Organization and its participating States:*

1. *Continue the practice of extended periods of service on protracted conflicts for Special Representatives of the Chairperson-in-Office (CiO).*

2. Increase Vienna-based support for such Special Representatives.
3. Enhance cross-institutional, cross-dimensional, and cross-conflict coordination and capacity building.
4. Strengthen the role and capacity of existing technical working groups below high-level negotiation formats and create new ones as need and opportunity dictate.
5. Use existing formats to facilitate confidence building among key OSCE participating States to create a geopolitical environment more conducive to the negotiations on protracted conflicts taking place.
6. Be realistic regarding what existing formats can currently accomplish and adjust goals flexibly in light of circumstances.
7. Assess whether existing negotiation formats have the potential, at least in the mid- to long-term to facilitate a settlement of protracted conflicts within the parameters of international law and the OSCE norm consensus.

## Introduction

Why do protracted conflicts in the post-Soviet space occur, why do they persist, and why do they matter? Why are the various negotiation formats and their track records important to know, even if they have so far been distinctly unimpressive? What are the revealing commonalities and differences between the different settlement process and their results?

The unresolved territorial conflicts in Eastern Europe are protracted, rather than frozen, meaning that there remains an acute danger of a resurgence of violence as happened, for example, in and around Nagorno-Karabakh in 2020. These conflicts provide Russia with geopolitical leverage beyond the concrete confrontation on the ground, while having extremely detrimental effects for the populations, states, and societies affected. This includes a persistent lack of political stability, greatly restrained economic development, large-scale human rights violations, etc.

As noted above, negotiated settlements are the stated preferred outcome for the overwhelming majority of the involved parties, despite their failure to materialized or to be implemented (as in the case of the Donbas). Nevertheless, the various negotiation formats, including those created ad hoc, have proved relevant. They have contributed to stabilizing volatile situations, providing humanitarian relief, and addressing issues short of political settlement, such as economic connectivity, freedom of movement, or environmental management. However, they have not brought the conflicts any closer to a resolution based on international law and OSCE principles and commitments.

## The Protracted Conflicts and Their Negotiation Formats

The negotiation formats in the five protracted conflicts examined here have a number of features in common, most strikingly perhaps the lack of accurately defined conflict parties and of progress towards a negotiated settlement. At the same time, there are important differences concerning the number of negotiations and the extent to which these have (not) led to a more stable and secure situation on the ground and (not) created an environment that is more conducive to future conflict settlement efforts.

In the case of the Transnistrian conflict in Moldova, the general lack of progress towards a settlement of the conflict must not be imputed to a lack of effort on the part of the various domestic and external actors. Numerous plans and strategies were elaborated, especially during the first decade of conflict settlement attempts.[2] Even during periods of high

---

2   S. Wolff, "A Resolvable Frozen Conflict? Designing a Settlement for Transnistria", *Nationalities Papers*, vol. 39, no. 6 (2011): 863-870, https://doi.org/10.1080/00905992.2011.617363.

tension between Chișinău and Tiraspol, or during geopolitical crises, communications between the two sides never broke down completely and were always maintained at least informally. Over the past decade, however, there has been a noticeable turn from efforts at conflict settlement towards stabilization of the status quo. This has manifested itself in a focus on so-called confidence-building measures (CBMs), which have tackled issues in such a way as to improve the functioning of existing arrangements without moving the conflict itself closer to a settlement.

The current 5+2 negotiation format emerged in 2005 when the EU and the US (+2) joined the existing five-sided format consisting of Moldova and the de facto authorities of the Transnistrian region, as the two conflict parties, plus the OSCE, Russia, and Ukraine as mediators and guarantors of a settlement. For more than a decade now, and arguably during the decade before, confidence building has been a constant feature within an otherwise inconclusive settlement process. This has also been facilitated by the flexibility of the 5+2 format, which in some ways also functions as an umbrella for formal and informal 1+1 talks (between the respective chief negotiators of Chișinău and Tiraspol), for discussions among the 3+2 (OSCE, Russia, Ukraine, the US, the EU), and for several more technical Working Groups co-chaired by deputy ministers from Moldova and their de facto Transnistrian region counterparts. This has meant that, although talks are often deadlocked at the highest political level, technical discussions can continue and prepare the ground for political decisions that could be made when there is a window of opportunity. Examples are the gradual, albeit still incomplete, implementation of the so-called called "Package of Eight" (or Berlin+ agreement), the successful 2015 Deep and Comprehensive Free Trade (DCFTA) negotiations for the secessionist Transnistrian region in the context of the annual so-called "Bavaria Conference", which represents yet another forum complementing the overall 5+2 format.

By contrast, Georgia's two protracted conflicts in Abkhazia and the Tskhinvali region ("South Ossetia"), the Russo-Georgian war of 2008 and Russia's subsequent recognition of the two separatist regions as states constituted a fundamental game changer in that they broke established principles of international law and challenged the OSCE's norm consensus. Until then, the UN and the OSCE had overseen settlement processes which were, however, highly unproductive and largely dysfunctional. In the aftermath of the 2008 Five-Day War, the Geneva International Discussions (GID) became the only forum in which Georgia, Russia, and the de facto representatives of Abkhazia and South Ossetia interact. They do so in fulfillment of the final point of the 2008 ceasefire agreement, namely to open "international discussions on the modalities of security and stability in Abkhazia and South Ossetia".[3]

The relative stability of the current status quo in the conflicts in Abkhazia and South Ossetia is based on Russia's "protection" of the conflict zones and their increasing integration with Russia. Although there has been some minimal progress over the years on a few humanitarian issues in the Geneva negotiations, there is no longer even the pretence of a conflict settlement process. The implementation plan for the Medvedev-Sarkozy six-point plan of 12 August 2008 establishes the scope of the GID merely "arrangements to ensure

---

3  Author's translation based on the French-language version of the six-point plan. The two Russian-language versions talk about "international discussions on the modalities of lasting security in South Ossetia and Abkhazia". See "Six-Point Peace Plan for the Georgia-Russia Conflict", *United Nations Peacemaker Database*, 2008, https://peacemaker.un.org/sites/peacemaker.un.org/files/GE_080812_Protocol d%27accord_0.pdf.

security and stability in the region; the issue of refugees and displaced persons on the basis of the internationally recognized principles and post-conflict settlement practice; any other subject, by mutual agreement of the parties".[4] With mutual agreement mostly absent, Georgian initiatives, like the Government's 2018 peace initiative, "A Step to a Better Future", and its offer of a unilateral commitment to the non-use of force have not been discussed in a manner that would pave the way to actual settlement negotiations.[5]

Regarding Nagorno-Karabakh, conflict settlement negotiations have been as fruitless as in the other three cases. The status quo here is one characterized by especially high volatility and virtually no prospect of sustainable stabilization, let alone progress towards a negotiated settlement. Following the renewed escalation of military hostilities in autumn 2020, the conflict over Nagorno-Karabakh has become structurally both more similar and more dissimilar to the other conflicts. Russia now has an established military presence on the ground along the ceasefire line and protects the land connection between Nagorno-Karabakh and Armenia. At the same time, Russia has managed to defend the existing Minsk Group format, and its dominant role within it, against Turkish attempts to create a new separate negotiation format.

---

4 "Implementation of the Plan of 12 August", United Nations Peacemaker Database, 2008, https://peacemaker.un.org/sites/peacemaker.un.org/files/GE_080909_Implementation of the 12 August 2008 Plan.pdf.

5 The 2018 peace initiative includes two separate policies on trade facilitation and on educational opportunities. See State Minister of Georgia for Reconciliation and Civic Equality, "'A Step to a Better Future' Peace Initiative Enhancing Educational Opportunities for the Residents of Abkhazia and Tskhinvali Region/South Ossetia", 2018, https://smr.gov.ge/uploads/prev/Education_ _9dd0e9dc.pdf; State Minister of Georgia for Reconciliation and Civic Equality, "'A Step to a Better Future' Peace Initiative Facilitation of Trade Across Dividing Lines", 2018, https://smr.gov.ge/uploads/prev/Concept_EN_0eaaa c2e.pdf.

A key difference is that representatives of the Nagorno-Karabakh authorities remain formally excluded and can only exercise varying degrees of influence on the Armenian position. There are so far also no significant Track 2 or Track 3 initiatives. Thus, to the extent that one can speak in any meaningful way about a settlement process at all, it is almost entirely driven externally, i.e. by the co-chairs of the OSCE Minsk Group and especially by Russia. Discussions are conducted only at the highest political levels in Yerevan and Baku.

Another telling peculiarity of the Nagorno-Karabakh negotiations is that all conceivable options, in terms of both the substance and the process of a settlement, have already been put on the table at some point. Yet they were all ultimately rejected by one of the two sides—or by both. The Package Plan, the Step by Step (or phased) approach, the Common State plan, a Land Swap proposal, and the Madrid Principles (or so-called "Basic Principles") have all suffered the same fate over the past two decades.

To be sure, the Madrid Principles, which represent a combination of more or less compatible preferences contained in the earlier Package Plan and phased approach, are formally still on the table. Yet there has been little progress towards an agreement since they were first suggested by the co-chairs of the OSCE Minsk Group. After the last "fruitless summit in Kazan in June 2011 ... the Minsk Group circled in a diplomatic wilderness".[6] Worse, it "went into a dormancy

---

6   L. Broers, "Requiem for the Unipolar Moment in Nagorny Karabakh", *Current History*, vol. 120, no. 828 (2021): 255-261, https://doi.org/10.1525/CURH.20 21.120.828.255.

that lasted through the Azerbaijani offensive of 2016, the Armenian revolution of 2018, and the 2020 fighting".[7]

After the 2020 military escalation and ceasefire agreement, which makes no provision for any settlement negotiations, there are no realistic prospects of positive change in this regard. This is despite the fact that, in their respective statements to the 2021 UN General Assembly, Azerbaijan's and Armenia's leaders proclaimed their willingness to engage in settlement negotiations. Ilham Aliyev noted that "Azerbaijan has already announced its readiness to embark upon the border delimitation and demarcation between Azerbaijan and Armenia, and to start negotiations on peace agreement [sic] with Armenia, based on mutual recognition of sovereignty and territorial integrity of each other [sic]".[8] Meanwhile, Nikol Pashinyan stated that "Armenia is ready for a constructive dialogue, which should lead to the establishment of sustainable and lasting peace in the region" and that it was "necessary to resume the peace process for the settlement of the Nagorno-Karabakh conflict under the auspices of the OSCE Minsk Group Co-Chairs". At the same time, however, both statements were openly hostile towards the other side.[9]

---

[7] P. Remler et al., "OSCE Minsk Group: Lessons from the Past and Tasks for the Future", *OSCE Insights,* no. 6 (2020): 85–99, https://doi.org/10.5771/9783848922339-06.

[8] I. Aliyev, "Statement by H.E. Mr. Ilham Aliyev, President of the Republic of Azerbaijan, to the General Debate of the 76th Session of the United Nations General Assembly", *United Nations,* 23 September 2021, https://estatements.unmeetings.org/estatements/10.0010/20210923/5DX0mCyb94TX/nuzzTkqSWaW9_en.pdf.

[9] N. Pashinyan, "Statement by H.E. Mr. Nikol Pashinyan, Prime Minister of Armenia, to the General Debate of the 76th Session of the United Nations General Assembly", *United Nations,* 24 September 2021, https://estatements.unmeetings.org/estatements/10.0010/20210924/7gIp44D6mxWV/Nn1M9CNhBEVL_en.pdf. For a more optimistic assessment, see Aylin Unver Noi, "Can 'make Trade Not War' Become a New Reality in the Caucasus?", *The Hill,* 27 September 2021, https://thehill.com/opinion/international/574099-can-make-trade-not-war-become-a-new-reality-in-the-caucasus.

The most recent protracted conflict is the one in Ukraine's Donbas region, which started in April 2014. After Moscow's instigation of a violent escalation, separatist forces, with active Russian participation and support, established two de facto states, the DNR and LNR.[10] A similar negotiation format soon emerged in the form of the so-called "Trilateral Contact Group", which includes Ukraine, the Russian Federation, and the OSCE, while representatives of the DNR and LNR are present in the working sub-groups. Similar to the 5+2 and the GID, these working groups deal with security, political, economic, and humanitarian issues.

As in the other cases, substantive progress in the negotiations has been limited, if not nonexistent. There were several successful prisoner exchanges, but recently talks on this matter have stalled again.[11] Freedom of movement across the "contact line" has become more rather than less constrained. Above all, there has been no material progress whatsoever towards implementation of the Minsk II Accords of February 2015. There has been no withdrawal of illegal armed groups and military equipment or of fighters and mercenaries from the territory of Ukraine (Minsk I); illegal groups have not been disarmed (Minsk II).

Regarding security, the Trilateral Contact Group concluded negotiations on a Framework Decision relating to disengagement of forces and hardware in September 2016. Its so far patchy implementation has been monitored by the

---

10  See T. Malyarenko and S. Wolff, "The Logic of Competitive Influence-Seeking: Russia, Ukraine, and the Conflict in Donbas", *Post-Soviet Affairs*, vol. 34, no. 4 (2018): 191–212, https://doi.org/10.1080/1060586X.2018.1425083; and J. Hauter, "Forensic Conflict Studies: Making Sense of War in the Social Media Age", *Media, War & Conflict*, 4 August 2021, https://doi.org/10.1177/17506352 211037325.
11  Organization for Security and Co-operation in Europe, "Press Statement of Special Representative Kinnunen after the Regular Meeting of Trilateral Contact Group on 26 August 2021", *OSCE*, 26 August 2021, https://www.osce.org/chairmanship/496483.

OSCE's Special Monitoring Mission, which, however, is prevented from monitoring all of the non-government-controlled areas, particularly the non-government-controlled Ukrainian-Russian state border, over which arms and fighters to the DNR/LNR travel from Russia.[12] The Trilateral Contact Group achieved an apparent breakthrough in July 2020 when negotiators "reached agreement regarding additional measures to strengthen the ceasefire, aiming to ensure compliance with a comprehensive, sustainable and unlimited ceasefire".[13] However, one year on from this agreement, the situation along the line of contact remains highly volatile. The number of daily ceasefire violations has risen again in the course of 2021 to levels similar to those prior to the July 2020 agreement.

Unlike the other cases discussed here, the conflict in eastern Ukraine is characterized by a second negotiation platform, the so-called "Normandy Format", which comprises Russia, Ukraine, France and Germany. In the early years of the conflict in Donbas, negotiations proved critical in achieving the two Minsk agreements of September 2014 and February 2015. Since then, further meetings of the four countries' leaders or their advisors have taken place on a semi-regular basis, but without any notable breakthrough regarding the stalled implementation of the Minsk II Accords. The last meeting of the Normandy Quartet at the highest level took place in Paris in December 2019 without any tangible

---

12 Organization for Security and Co-operation in Europe, "Framework Decision of the Trilateral Contact Group Relating to Disengagement of Forces and Hardware", *OSCE*, 20 September 2016, https://www.osce.org/files/f/documents/2/4/266271.pdf.
13 Organization for Security and Co-operation in Europe, "Press Statement of Special Representative Grau after the Regular Meeting of Trilateral Contact Group on 22 July 2020", *OSCE*, 23 July 2020, https://www.osce.org/chairmanship/457885.

results.¹⁴ Since then discussions regarding another such meeting have proven largely fruitless.¹⁵

## Insights from Three Decades of Negotiations: What Has (Not) Worked and Why?

In four of the five protracted conflicts covered here, negotiations have been ongoing for around three decades now. In the fifth case, that of Ukraine, they are less than a decade old. Despite the considerable resources spent by all sides involved, none of the conflicts has moved closer to a solution. Even preserving the stability of the status quo seems hard to accomplish at the negotiation table, as the 2008 Russo-Georgian and 2020 Armenian-Azerbaijani wars vividly illustrated.

## Agreement on Non-political Issues Is Possible

Despite the notable absence of any breakthroughs on political status issues, negotiations have not been completely useless. In particular, non-political issues tended to have a good chance of being negotiated and implemented. That was especially the case if they contributed to improving economic and

---

14 During the summit, its members managed to agree a prisoner swap, but made otherwise no real progress other than "underlin[ing] their common aspiration for a comprehensive and sustainable architecture of trust and security in Europe, based on the principles of the OSCE, of which the resolution of the conflict in Ukraine is one of the important steps". See "Agreed Conclusions of the Paris Summit of the Normandy Format", 9 December 2019, https://www.elysee.fr/emmanuel-macron/2019/12/09/sommet-de-paris-en-format-normandie. See also K. Gorchinskaya, "The Normandy Summit Ended With No Breakthroughs. What Has It Achieved?" *Forbes*, 10 December 2019, https://www.forbes.com/sites/katyagorchinskaya/2019/12/10/the-normandy-summit-ended-what-has-it-achieved/; and M. Minakov, "Results of the Normandy Format Talks for Ukraine: Hope, with Reservations", *Ukraine Focus*, December 11, 2019, https://www.wilsoncenter.org/blog-post/results-the-normandy-format-talks-for-ukraine-hope-reservations.
15 "Berlin Says Leaders Of Germany, France, Ukraine, Russia Agree To Ministerial-Level Meeting", Radio Free Europe/Radio Liberty, 11 October 2021, https://www.rferl.org/a/31504107.html.

social development, freedom of movement, access to services, humanitarian relief, and other issues from which the immediate conflict parties, as well as their external patrons, benefitted. This has been evident in the cases of Transnistria, pre-2008 Abkhazia (and, to a lesser extent, South Ossetia),[16] as well as Donbas.[17]

In the case of Transnistria, the Package of Eight has achieved some results. Initially agreed in Berlin in June 2016 during the German CiO,[18] significant further progress was made under the Austrian and Italian CiOs in 2017[19] and 2018.[20] By May 2019, negotiations on six out of the eight priority issues agreed in Berlin in June 2016 had been concluded successfully. This included the opening of the Gura Bicului–Bychok bridge and acceptance of Transnistrian license plates. However, this confidence building process did not continue

---

16  See P. Remler, "Protracted Conflicts in the OSCE Area: Innovative Approaches for Co-Operation in the Conflict Zones" (Hamburg, 2016), http://osce-netwo rk.net/file-OSCE-Network/documents/Protracted_Conflicts_OSCE_WEB.pdf and S. Wolff, P. Remler, and L. Davies, "OSCE Confidence Building in the Economic and Environmental Dimension: Current Opportunities and Constraints" (Hamburg, 2017), http://osce-network.net/file-OSCE-Network/ Publications/OSCE_Confidence_Building_in_EED_final.pdf.

17  The OSCE Special Monitoring Mission has regularly facilitated local ceasefires to repair and maintain critical civilian infrastructure. See, for example, Special Monitoring Mission to Ukraine, "SMM Facilitation and Monitoring of Infrastructure Repair in Eastern Ukraine", *OSCE*, 2019, https://www.osce.org /files/f/documents/f/2/437834.pdf.

18  Organization for Security and Co-operation in Europe, "Protocol of the Official Meeting of the Permanent Conference for Political Questions in the Framework of the Negotiating Process on the Transdniestrian Settlement, 2-3 June 2016, Berlin", *OSCE*, June 2016, https://www.osce.org/files/f/documents/d/f/244 656.pdf.

19  Organization for Security and Co-operation in Europe, "Ministerial Statement on the Negotiations on the Transdniestrian Settlement Process in the '5+2' Format", *OSCE*, 8 December 2017, https://www.osce.org/files/f/documents /a/c/361586.pdf.

20  Organization for Security and Co-operation in Europe, "Ministerial Statement on the Negotiations on the Transdniestrian Settlement Process in the '5+2' Format", *OSCE*, 7 December 2018, https://www.osce.org/files/f/documents /b/2/405917.pdf.

under the subsequent Slovak,[21] Albanian,[22] and Swedish CiOs.[23]

Such ambivalent successes are often associated with a lack of alternatives to local accommodation. For example, Transnistria has no border with Russia, and thus depends on viable arrangements with Chișinău and Kyiv to ensure the continued ability of its residents to travel and its businesses to import and export goods. Similarly, Donbas depends on cooperation with Kyiv for the continued functioning of critical civilian infrastructure, especially related to water and electricity supplies. The same was true for South Ossetia in the early post-2008 period, when there were no realistic alternatives for gas supplies via the Agara-Tskhinvali pipeline or for the maintenance of the Zonkari dam serving communities on both sides of the administrative boundary line.[24] Over the years, however, South Ossetia has become less dependent on

---

21 Organization for Security and Co-operation in Europe, "Ministerial Statement on the Negotiations on the Transdniestrian Settlement Process in the '5+2' Format", OSCE, 6 December 2019, https://www.osce.org/files/f/documents/9/8/441524.pdf.
22 Organization for Security and Co-operation in Europe, "Ministerial Statement on the Negotiations on the Transdniestrian Settlement Process in the '5+2' Format", OSCE, 4 December 2020, https://www.osce.org/files/f/documents/4/4/479774.pdf.
23 Organization for Security and Co-operation in Europe, "Joint Statement by the Mediators and the Observers in the Permanent Conference on Political Issues in the Framework of the Negotiation Process on the Transdniestrian Settlement in the 5+2 Format Following Their 3-4 June 2021 Visit to Chisinau and Tiraspol", OSCE, 4 June 2021, https://www.osce.org/chairmanship/488530. See also "OSCE Chairperson-in-Office Linde Concludes Visit to Moldova", Organization for Security and Co-operation in Europe, 6 October 2021, https://www.osce.org/chairmanship/499948.
24 T. Giuashvili and J. Devdariani, "Geneva International Discussions – Negotiating the Possible", *Security and Human Rights*, vol. 27, nos. 3-4, 16 September2016): 381-402, https://doi.org/10.1163/18750230-02703003.

such cooperation initiatives,[25] and there have been no parallel "easy wins" of late.[26]

By contrast, neither Armenia nor Nagorno-Karabakh had, at least until 2020, any constraints at all and hence only a limited need for engaging even on relatively non-political issues. Given the new realities on the ground after the 2020 war, especially Armenia's loss of control over the territories surrounding the Lachin corridor, this may gradually change and require a higher level of engagement between Armenia and the authorities in Nagorno-Karabakh and Azerbaijan. This could create openings for more purposeful OSCE engagement, whether through the Minsk Group, the Conflict Prevention Centre, or the CiO.[27]

However, difficulties also emerge in the opposite direction. An isolationist policy pursued by the metropolitan state and also the international community can reduce the possibilities of even limited engagement by authorities in breakaway regions. Higher reliance, and subsequently dependence, on the patron state may be a consequence. It may mean increased leverage for the patron state over the breakaway

---

25 For example, since the opening of the Dzuarikau-Tskhinvali pipeline in 2009, South Ossetia no longer depends on gas transits via Georgia.
26 For example, the Odzisi crossing point at the Georgia-South Ossetia administrative boundary line has been closed for more than two years, severely restricting the freedom of movement of people on both sides. See Organization for Security and Co-operation in Europe, "102nd Incident Prevention and Response Mechanism Meeting Takes Place in Ergneti", *OSCE*, 27 September 2021, https://www.osce.org/chairmanship/499005.
27 Remler et al., "OSCE Minsk Group: Lessons from the Past and Tasks for the Future".

authorities, as illustrated by the case of Abkhazia.[28] Once established, such dependencies are difficult to break.[29]

Another reason why agreements are, at times, possible is because de facto authorities in the conflict zones, on occasion, have a brief window of opportunity in which they can exercise relative situational autonomy. Gains made in these periods are more likely to be sustained if they do not touch on (final) status questions but rather consolidate an already established status quo, one serving often deeply entrenched constituents on both sides. Thus, Moldovan and de facto Transnistrian negotiators agreed on an Agenda and on Principles & Procedures for their settlement talks in 2012.[30] Yet they have so far not started negotiations on the so-called third basket (final status questions).

Situational autonomy was facilitated by rapprochement between Russia and the EU in the context of the 2010 Meseberg process. Initial progress in the 5+2 talks in 2011–2012, after a five-year hiatus, also benefitted from regime change in Chișinău (2009) and Tiraspol (2011). Yet the resurgent geopolitical rivalry between the US and Russia after Putin's resumption of the Russian presidency in 2012, the failure of the US "reset", and the intensification of EU-Moldova negotiations on an Association Agreement meant that the

---

28  See, for example, A. Gegeshidze, "Prospects for Abkhazia's De-Isolation in the Context of the Non-Recognition Policy", in *The De-Isolation of Abkhazia*, edited by International Alert (London: International Alert, 2011), 27–37, https://www.international-alert.org/sites/default/files/Caucasus_DeIsolationOfAbkhazia_EN_2011.pdf; L. Kvarchelia, "Sanctions and the Path Away from Peace", in *Powers of Persuasion: Incentives, Sanctions and Conditionality in Peacemaking*, edited by Aaron Griffiths and Catherine Barnes (London: Conciliation Resources, 2008), 71–73, https://www.c-r.org/accord/incentives-sanctions-and-conditionality/sanctions-and-path-away-peace.

29  T. de Waal, "Abkhazia: Stable Isolation", *Carnegie Europe*, 3 December 2018, https://carnegieeurope.eu/2018/12/03/abkhazia-stable-isolation-pub-77842.

30  Organization for Security and Co-operation in Europe, "OSCE Chairperson Hails Breakthrough in Transdniestrian Settlement Talks", *OSCE*, 18 April 2012, https://www.osce.org/cio/89764.

OSCE-facilitated settlement process slowed down during 2012. It ground to a complete halt after the escalation of the conflict in Ukraine.[31]

By contrast, in late 2015, Chișinău, Tiraspol, and the EU reached an agreement on the application of the DCFTA to Transnistria, which has held ever since.[32] This was partly a result of Moscow not blocking engagement between Tiraspol and Brussels and tolerating its result. This provided the Transnistrian de facto authorities with a certain situational autonomy in the negotiations. Equally important was the fact that there were important Track 2 initiatives involving representatives from the Moldovan and Transnistrian chambers of commerce, NGOs, and academics, such as a project on developing cross-river trade relations, supported by the UK's Conflict, Stability, and Security Fund. They ran in parallel to official negotiations on the DCFTA and added some pressure from business communities.

Such broader social traction is critical and its absence detrimental. In the case of Nagorno-Karabakh, for example, these kinds of initiatives, to the limited extent that they exist at all, are constrained by the restrictive approaches of the two governments. They are also hindered by deep antagonism between the societies of both countries and of Nagorno-Karabakh. When initiatives happen, they occur predominantly in third countries and involve a small number of actors, often with no lasting positive impact. This, in turn, has had a significant negative impact on the preparedness for compromise and concessions on all sides and has led to the

---

31 J. Beyer and S. Wolff, "Linkage and Leverage Effects on Moldova's Transnistria Problem", *East European Politics*, vol. 32, no. 3 (2016): 335–354, https://doi.org/10.1080/21599165.2015.1124092.

32 N. Douglas and S. Wolff, "Economic Confidence-Building Measures and Conflict Settlement: The Case of Transdniestria" (Berlin, 2018), https://stefanwolff.com/wp-content/uploads/2021/05/Douglas-and-Wolff-Economic-Confidence-Building-Measures-and-Conflict-Settlement.pdf.

entrenchment of mutually exclusive and, for the most part, openly hostile narratives about the conflict, its causes, and possible solutions.

## Success on Non-political Issues Does Not (Automatically) Spill over into Political Issue Areas and Does Not (Necessarily) Prevent a Resurgence of Violence

Local and geopolitical conditions permitting, confidence built in the context of agreements on non-political issues contributes more broadly to stabilization and has some positive spill-over effects into non-economic areas of confidence building.[33] Yet this effect is often limited and has not yet paved the way to a sustainable negotiated settlement in any of the cases considered here. In the case of Transnistria, for example, we have seen almost three decades of relative progress on relevant non-political issues, through the extensive use of CBMs. Yet the conflict is hardly any closer to a settlement than it was in the 1990s. Similarly, prisoner exchanges in Ukraine since 2014, and between Armenia and Azerbaijan after the 2020 escalation of hostilities, have not contributed to any political progress.

Nor does success on such non-political issues necessarily prevent conflict re-escalation. There was a reasonable level of "non-political progress" related to Abkhazia and South Ossetia. However, this was swept away during and even in the run-up to the 2008 Russo-Georgian war. An important difference from the case of Transnistria was that access to the two conflict zones was limited by the local authorities and by a

---

[33] N. Kemoklidze and S. Wolff, "Trade as a Confidence-Building Measure in Protracted Conflicts: The Cases of Georgia and Moldova Compared", *Eurasian Geography and Economics*, vol. 61, no. 3 (2020): 305–332, https://doi.org/10.1080/15387216.2019.1702567.

relatively restrictive Georgian policy on the operation of NGOs in Abkhazia and South Ossetia. This meant that Track 2 and Track 3 initiatives have by far not had the same reach or impact as in the Transnistrian case and that their overall impact was significantly lower. This was true in the case of the forced closure of the Ergneti market in 2004. Confidence destroyed by such actions is difficult to rebuild and its loss can lead to violence.

Across all the cases considered here, with the exception of Nagorno-Karabakh, top-level negotiation formats tend to be complemented by parallel technical, working or/and expert groups that address specific issues, often outside of the political limelight, and with less pressure from political leaders. This not only facilitates success on non-political issues. It can also prepare the ground for spill-over effects in other issue areas. As illustrated by the case of Transnistria, this is a relatively low-risk and low-cost endeavor. A potentially high-gain strategy may well be driven by short-term, pragmatic considerations on both sides.

For instance, in the process of engagement, expert groups in Moldova have contributed to creating new patterns of practice and expectations and created a space for various Track 2 and Track 3 initiatives that bring various civil society actors into the process. Among the latter are the so-called "Transnistrian Dialogues" and the Annual Moldovan European Integration Forum, as well more ad hoc projects like the above-mentioned 2015 British-sponsored initiative to facilitate engagement between relevant actors in Chișinău and Tiraspol allowing them to map out options for the application of DCFTA to Transnistria.

Often sector- and audience-specific in their objectives, such initiatives, externally sponsored and often framed as CBMs, have created an environment in which broad engagement between different actors is possible and constructive. Nevertheless, this environment is not immune to political pressure. The political situation in Transnistria has become more oppressive over the past five years. The polarization in Moldovan society sometimes constrains the ability (and willingness) of political and civil society actors there to engage with the other side.

Similarly, the ups and downs of the two Incident Prevention and Response Mechanisms (IPRMs) set up in Georgia, in the context of the GID—IPRM Ergneti (facilitated by the EU and the OSCE) and IPRM Gali (facilitated by the EU and the UN)—demonstrate both the potential and vulnerability of such CBMs and the mechanisms used to implement them. IPRM Ergneti was commended for facilitating "effective co-operation ... during the irrigation season that resolved concrete issues regarding access to water".[34] On the other hand, IPRM Gali is currently under a second lengthy suspension (starting in 2018, after an earlier hiatus between 2012 and 2016).

The broader contribution that CBMs have made, however, is undeniable. This is most obvious in the Transnistrian case where they have shaped a status quo that has remained stable for a long period of time. This status quo represents a baseline for both sides (and arguably for external actors as well) which they are unlikely to be willing to lose. At the same time, it represents an increasingly solid foundation from which progress towards a final status settlement might be possible. But even if such efforts prove futile, the alternative is not a return to conflict, but the continuation of the status quo shaped by CBMs which at least partly reflects the

---

34 Organization for Security and Co-operation in Europe, "102nd Incident Prevention and Response Mechanism Meeting Takes Place in Ergneti".

sides' core concerns and, as such, does not entice them to resume violence.

## For Settlements to Be Sustainable, They Need to Be Negotiated by the Conflict Parties

Certain important lessons can be drawn concerning the aim of the status settlements that have so far eluded negotiators in all of the cases considered here. The first point to make is that such settlements cannot be imposed from the outside. The Minsk Accords are unlikely ever to be implemented. Multiple external proposals for Nagorno-Karabakh have not led to an actual settlement.

Second, status settlements will not gain societal traction if they are perceived to be favored by, or favoring, just one side (and its external backers) in a conflict. This applies to the Minsk Accords again, but also to the Kozak Memorandum of 2003 and the Georgian proposal for autonomy for South Ossetia of 2005. A third point is that "as important as the right institutional design and the correctly timed, designed and well-resourced international engagement may be, they cannot make up for shortcomings in local leadership. In other words, conflict management in divided societies cannot succeed unless there is a genuine commitment to peace among the parties to such conflicts".[35]

Third, there should be an acknowledgment that the conflict parties are not composed simply of the de facto authorities in separatist entities and the governments of their metropolitan states. With the partial exception of Nagorno-Karabakh, the OSCE region's protracted conflicts are deeply

---

35 C. Yakinthou and S. Wolff, "Introduction", in *Conflict Management in Divided Societies: Theories and Practice*, edited by Stefan Wolff and Christalla Yakinthou (London and New York: Routledge, 2013), 1–20, https://doi.org/10.4324/9780203803004.

embedded in geopolitical rivalries between Russia and the West. The struggle over zones of influence, reminiscent of the Cold War, is also conducted in the negotiation formats of these conflicts. Consequently, so-called mediators and guarantors pursue their own goals in and through these formats. To the degree that they thereby also become parties to the conflict, no negotiated settlement on the ground will be possible or sustainable unless efforts are made to at least mitigate these geopolitical tensions.

## Conclusions

There is no alternative to negotiated settlements, whatever their specific institutional design. Yet status negotiations are not always productive or even feasible. Hence, confidence- and security-building measures (CSBMs)/CBMs can be a useful means to manage conflicts as long as their limited function—i.e. conflict management rather than settlement—is acknowledged and there are realistic expectations as to their results. They should be supported and facilitated by the OSCE and its participating States. At the same time, the ground for any final settlement needs to be prepared carefully, including at the elite level. Whatever is eventually negotiated should be feasible—i.e. adoptable by political leaders and acceptable within societies/ratification processes—and viable, i.e. sustainable in the long term.

Achieving such a degree of preparedness also requires a structure of negotiation formats diverse enough to allow for compartmentalized negotiations on different matters without thereby proliferating formats themselves. Moreover, negotiation formats need to be constantly validated through at least some tangible outcomes. The alternative—prolonged periods of non-outcomes—creates the temptation of a recourse to violence and/or the establishment of separate, parallel formats for negotiations.

CSBMs and CBMs play a crucial role in conflict stabilization. Yet, when successful they also stabilize and entrench a status quo—a result that makes conflict settlement less urgent. Hence, they need to be structured in such a way that they do not foreclose future settlement opportunities. That means, for instance, that they can lead to a settlement creating a situation which is worse than the status quo for one or both sides. Therefore, confidence building needs to be characterized by mutuality, reciprocity, expandability, and retractability.

CSBMs/CBMs also need long-term financial security and political support from the "outside" to avoid stalling and blow-back. This requires multi-year strategic, financial and personnel frameworks. It also implies greater intra-OSCE and inter-organizational cooperation and coordination, including with established OSCE partners, such as the EU, the Council of Europe, the Shanghai Cooperation Organization, and the Conference on Interaction and Confidence-Building Measures in Asia.[36]

The protracted conflicts in the OSCE region are heavily influenced by geopolitical dynamics, especially the relationship between Russia and the West, which habitually accuse each other of instrumentalizing the protracted conflicts for their own strategic interests in the contested post-Soviet region. With the various dialogue formats now effectively constituting a "continuation of war by political means", the OSCE (at level of the Secretary-General and the CiO/Troika) needs carefully to manage different aspects of its mandate

---

36  D. Galbreath, A. Härtel, and S. Wolff, "Towards a More Strategic Partnership: Strengthening the OSCE through Enhanced EU–OSCE Cooperation", *OSCE Insights*, 14 April 2021, 1–11, https://doi.org/10.5771/9783748911456-03.

with regard to inter-state and intra-state relations. This should include a focus on comprehensive security that prioritizes, where necessary, humanitarian and economic aspects over political status issues, or at least "compartmentalizes" negotiations on different issues without making progress in one area conditional on progress elsewhere. Even small steps made on non-political issues are preferable to no steps at all and to the erosion of security and stability, or further polarization and radicalization by one or both sides and their external backers.

The geopolitical dimension of all the protracted conflicts examined here is further complicated by the fact that Russia is in fact a direct conflict party in three of the conflicts (Donbas, Abkhazia and South Ossetia) and holds the key to the resolution of another (Transnistria). Moreover, Moscow has just established a military presence on the ground in the last (Nagorno-Karabakh). Clearly, there is a larger Georgian-Russian and Ukrainian-Russian conflict level that needs to be addressed. Yet this should not distract from the fact that the local conflicts in Abkhazia and South Ossetia, as well as in the Donbas, require a sustainable intra-national settlement.

The trick is thus not to reduce preparatory confidence building to simply the local level, but rather to ensure that confidence is restored and maintained between otherwise rival geopolitical powers in the interest of security and stability in the OSCE region. The OSCE Minsk Group and especially the co-chair arrangement, the less-institutionalized 3+2 format within the 5+2 negotiation process, and the inconclusive Meseberg process of 2010-2012 offer instructive examples. The Normandy Format, although helpful in the early stages of the Donbas conflict, appears to have developed into a parallel and largely deadlocked mechanism that can no longer provide positive impulses to on-the-ground engagement through the Trilateral Contact Group.

Ultimately, the perception that the key to the settlement of the OSCE region's protracted conflicts lies with Russia is not wrong, but there is more to the persistent lack of settlement than Russian obstruction. Arguing otherwise simply absolves local conflict parties, observers, mediators, and the OSCE as a whole of any responsibility for decades of negotiations with few, if any, tangible results. It also creates the erroneous, and dangerous, impression that if Moscow were to drop its resistance tomorrow, the parties on the ground would happily and readily embrace a just and fair settlement of their differences on the basis of international law and OSCE consensus.

Russia has clearly played a role in instigating the conflict in Donbas, but the conflicts in Moldova, Georgia, and between Azerbaijan and Armenia were "home-made" in their origins. In other words, Russian policy is a significant but not unique reason for the protracted nature of the conflicts, and this is different from attributing the causes of these conflicts or the absence of any settlement to Russia alone.

Decades of lack of progress have created entrenched interests on all sides in the non-settlement of the protracted conflicts and/or in settlements that are neither feasible nor viable. In this sense, the existing negotiation formats, by merely simulating conflict settlement negotiations, have lost their sense of purpose and their sense of what an actual settlement of any of the protracted conflicts should look like. Even if this situation is in Russia's interest, it has been enabled, or at least not been sufficiently resisted, by others involved. It has, however, become a problem for the OSCE as a whole and can, therefore, only be solved by the OSCE as a whole in the original "Helsinki spirit".

## Recommendations

On the basis of the foregoing analysis, the following recommendations can be made.

1. **Continue the practice of extended periods of service of CiO Special Representatives.** Special Representatives of the CiO are independently appointed by the CiO and hence do not need an additional mandate from the OSCE Permanent Council. This takes their appointment out of the quasi-habitual wrangling over other similar positions. However, the potential downside is the extremely limited timeframe within which they can operate due to the annual rotation in the CiO. The notable exception to this has been the Personal Representative of the Chairperson-in-Office on the Conflict Dealt with by the OSCE Minsk Conference, based in Tbilisi, Georgia, a position held by Ambassador Andrzej Kasprzyk since 1997. There have now also been positive precedents of multi-annual appointments such as Angelo Gnaedinger, who served as the Special Representative of the OSCE CiO for the South Caucasus in 2014 and 2015, Günther Bächler. Who held the same post in 2016 and 2017, Franco Frattini, who served as the Special Representative of the OSCE CiO for the Transnistrian Settlement Process in 2018 and 2019, and Thomas Mayr-Harting, who has held this post since 2020. Such long-term appointments create opportunities for individuals to acquire more personal expertise regarding their portfolio, to build relationships with their various interlocutors among the conflict parties and mediators, and allows them to formulate and implement more coherent strategies regarding the conflicts they are dealing with.

2. **Increase Vienna-based support for Special Representatives.** Special Representatives with long-term mandates will still require increased support within the Secretariat to be effective and fulfill the potential that comes with longer

terms. Given the constrained budget of the Organization as a whole, including the Secretariat, additional commitments from participating States, including ad hoc "coalitions of friends" may be required to create the foundations for enhanced support. This could take the form of a small pool of geographical and subject matter experts that would serve all Special Representatives simultaneously, thereby also facilitating cross-conflict learning and sharing of best practices. This would also create continuities in knowledge and understanding that would support smooth transitions between Special Representatives regardless of the length of their term of office.

**3. Enhance cross-institutional, cross-dimensional, and cross-conflict coordination and capacity building.** In line with the idea of a Vienna-based support group for Special Representatives, more efforts should be made to enhance coordination regarding management of the protracted conflicts within the OSCE, involving institutions like the Office for Democratic Institutions and Human Rights (ODIHR) and the High Commissioner on National Minorities (HCNM) in conflict management activities. This would allow drawing on expertise in the Secretariat from each of the three dimensions of the OSCE and the creation of opportunities for peer learning across different conflict settings. ODIHR and HCNM expertise could, for example, be leveraged as a part of the Vienna-based support group, which might additionally include other experts, for example from the Office of the Co-ordinator of OSCE Economic and Environmental Activities. This would make better use of available expertise within OSCE institutions, create synergies between different types of conflict management activities, and contribute to building sustainable capacity within the Organization. Another dimension of this approach would be closer cooperation with other international organizations, for example in the context of regular consultations and operational cooperation between the OSCE and the EU. This would also provide a potential source of funding for the proposed capacity building within the OSCE, including through the secondment of personnel to a Vienna-based support group for the Special Representatives. Such secondments need not be limited to the EU or its member states.

4. **Strengthen the role and capacity of existing technical working groups below high-level negotiation formats and create new ones as need and opportunity dictate.** One of the key insights from the comparative analysis above concerns the utility of technical working groups to deal with specific, often non-political issues whose resolution can have tangible benefits for conflict-affected populations. For example, in relation to the Nagorno-Karabakh conflict, it should be assessed whether the Minsk Group could establish such formats to help the parties formalize and regularize their engagements. A good starting point would be working groups on second-dimension issues, including trade, access to services, and freedom of movement across the boundary line between the sides.

5. **Use existing formats to facilitate confidence building among key OSCE participating States to create a more conducive geopolitical environment for negotiations on protracted conflicts.** Given the significance of geopolitical tensions in the management of protracted conflicts, confidence building needs also to address the relationships between the OSCE participating States that are immediate stakeholders in the conflict. An obvious issue in this regard is the relationship with Russia. Here, the OSCE, and existing formats like the Minsk Group co-chairs and the 3+2 format in the Transnistrian settlement process, offer potential

opportunities for engagement. Additionally, involving Russian experts in the aforementioned enhanced support structures for Special Representatives would create additional channels of communication. The key objective of any such engagement should be to determine the parameters for OSCE conflict management, including mediation of ongoing negotiations, that have the endorsement of key stakeholders, including Russia. This might mean limiting, at least temporarily, the scope of OSCE conflict management, but would also imply the possibility of tangible progress on concrete issues that contribute to security and stability without infringing OSCE values and principles.

**6. Be realistic regarding what existing formats can currently accomplish and adjust goals flexibly in light of circumstances.** Even with the aforementioned steps, and potentially others, taken to strengthen OSCE capacity for the management of protracted conflicts in the OSCE area, it is important to be realistic about what can be accomplished within the existing dialogue formats. This is not a call to radically change, let alone replace these formats, but to manage expectations within the Organization and among its participating States. Breakthroughs to negotiated settlements are unlikely for the time being. Thus, current efforts should be directed at stabilization and the gradual improvement of the humanitarian situation. This can only be achieved within the context of functioning channels of communication in the existing dialogue formats, which in turn depend on not pushing conflict parties to negotiate on issues they are not willing to engage on. Rather, a gradual approach of small steps towards improving the situation on the ground builds confidence among the parties and mediators, without foreclosing future opportunities to negotiate issues that are currently too sensitive to touch. In turn, this creates a space for flexible responses to immediate needs on the ground and incentives for the conflict parties to remain constructively engaged in the existing dialogue formats.

**7. Assess whether existing negotiation formats have the potential, at least in the mid- to long-term, to facilitate a settlement of protracted conflicts within the parameters of international law and the OSCE norm consensus.** In light of a greater realism about what the existing formats can currently accomplish, it is also worth considering whether they are at all able to facilitate any settlement of the conflicts. After decades of negotiations and confidence building during which stabilization has been the closest thing to success that the OSCE has achieved, and even that with only a patchy track record, the question arises whether existing formats have become part of what makes these conflicts protracted. However, this question cannot be answered without greater clarity about what a settlement of any of the protracted conflicts, one that would respect international law and reaffirm the OSCE norm consensus, would look like. Importantly, this may not be a single "solution" but rather a menu of different options. It would then be left to negotiators to determine which of these is the most fitting for their specific circumstances.

*Dr. Stefan Wolff is Professor of International Security at the University of Birmingham in the UK.*

# Achievements and Limitations of the OSCE's Special Monitoring Mission in Ukraine's Donbas since 2014*

*Andreas Umland*

DOI: https://doi.org/10.24216/9783838216881_008

## Executive Summary

*Since the end of the Cold War, international organizations have struggled to fulfil the high hopes placed in them as backbones of a new rules-based world order, in particular the vision of an inclusive and peaceful European security order based on the Helsinki Final Act and the Paris Charter. The Organization for Security and Co-operation in Europe (OSCE) Special Monitoring Mission (SMM) to Ukraine has become a critical instrument of multilateral attempts to observe, manage and eventually resolve the Russian-Ukrainian conflict in the eastern Donbas since 2014. This report briefly illustrates how this conflict has posed an especially complicated challenge to consensus-based intergovernmental institutions such as the OSCE, which have become increasingly characterized by internal normative divergences. Russian obstruction and the inability of the OSCE to properly define and label the confrontation an armed interstate conflict between two of its participating states have resulted in serious limitations on what a mission such as the SMM can achieve. Despite the limits placed on it by Moscow's constraints and the lack of sufficient resources, the SMM has contributed significantly to de-escalation in the Donbas. Among other things, the SMM has preserved a notable presence on the spot, improved its reporting on the situation in the conflict zone and employed increasingly sophisticated monitoring methodologies and technologies. Nonetheless, the report recommends a number of further improvements to increase the SMM's effectiveness, and thereby facilitate an eventual solution to the conflict.*

## Introduction

Since 2014, the Organization for Security and Cooperation in Europe (OSCE) has been playing a central role in attempts to resolve of the Russian-Ukrainian conflict in the Donets' Basin (Donbas), above all by virtue of its especially large and sophisticated Special Monitoring Mission (SMM). The OSCE is also the crucial mediator at the negotiation table of the Trilateral Contact Group (TCG), which until recently had been meeting in Minsk. The OSCE Chairperson-in-Office sends, and provides the mandate for, a Special Representative to the TCG, which comprises Russia, Ukraine and the OSCE.

In collaboration with the Normandy Four Format (which is not dealt with in detail here), the OSCE sets the dominant institutional context, among other things through its Permanent Council, for multilateral attempts to resolve the conflict between Russia and Ukraine. Certain relatively new technologies in the context of such a mission, such as unmanned aerial vehicles (UAVs), satellites and long-range cameras, have been used on an unusually large scale in Ukraine, making the SMM the world's leading operation of its type. Against this backdrop, inferences drawn from the Ukrainian case have wider implications for civilian missions by international organizations elsewhere.[1]

---

\* This report relies on, among other things, a number of informal conversations with previous or current SMM and other OSCE officers whose kind but anonymous assistance is gratefully acknowledged. It also heavily draws on a 2020 research paper focused on the Ukrainian critique of the SMM, co-written by Umland with Dr. André Härtel (Institute for Peace Research and Security Policy, Hamburg) as well as Anton Pisarenko (Institute for Euro-Atlantic Cooperation, Kyiv). That longer article "The OSCE's Special Monitoring Mission to Ukraine" is forthcoming in the journal *Security and Human Rights* (Brill/Nijhoff) in 2021, and was produced, in 2019-2021, within the project "Collective Action

## The Mandate and Role of the SMM in the Minsk Negotiations

Established even before the outbreak of the first armed confrontations in the Donbas in mid-April 2014, the OSCE SMM is the only international monitoring group permanently deployed not only to the conflict area, but throughout Ukraine. The Mission has had only limited ground access to critical areas of the de facto occupied, non-government-controlled territories (see below) and has occasionally also been constrained in its access to certain installations in the government-controlled areas.[2] Nonetheless, it is by far the most important international actor on the ground, and acquired this position early on. The first monitors were deployed less than 24 hours after a consensual decision by all the OSCE participating states to establish the SMM on 21 March 2014.[3]

According to the Mission's original and, as of May 2021, still valid mandate, its aim is "to contribute ... to reducing tensions and fostering peace, stability and security; and to monitoring and supporting the implementation of all OSCE principles and commitments".[4] The SMM has an annual budget of over €100 million, which in OSCE terms is a significant amount. The entire OSCE Unified Budget, which excludes

---

of Non-State Armed Groups in the Ukrainian Conflict: A Comparison of Pro-Russian and Ukrainian Non-state Armed Groups" funded by the Volkswagen Foundation in Germany. See: app.dimensions.ai/details/grant/grant.4974241.
1 H. Dijkstra, P. Petrov and E. Mahr, "Learning to Deploy Civilian Capabilities: How the United Nations, Organization for Security and Co-operation in Europe and European Union Have Changed Their Crisis Management Institutions", *Cooperation and Conflict*, vol. 54, no. 4 (2019): 524-543.
2 A. Hug, "Pikuzy: koly zblyzhennia tilky viddaliaie", *Dzerkalo Tyzhnia*, 3 November 2017, https://dt.ua/SOCIUM/osin-pikuzi-inshiy-svit-259076_.html (accessed 1 October 2019).
3 J. Engvall, "OSCE and Military-Confidence Building in Conflicts: Lessons from Georgia and Ukraine", *FOI Report*, no. 4750 (2019): 40.
4 "Permanent Council Decision No. 1117", *OSCE*, 21 March 2014, https://www.osce.org/pc/116747 (accessed 4 April 2020).

the SMM, in 2019, for instance, was €138,204,100. Nonetheless, the SMM is still a comparatively cheap operation in comparison with many United Nations peacekeeping operations. The SMM has in recent years had approximately 1,300 staff members, among whom more than 700 are monitors who not only observe developments on the spot, but also work to reduce tensions within the ongoing conflict.[5]

The nature and shape of the SMM differs from previous and other currently operating OSCE missions. A former member of the SMM, Hilde Haug has, among other things, highlighted that "it was the first time that the OSCE deployed a civilian field mission of this scope that would come to work in a high-risk environment in an active conflict stage".[6] By early 2020, for instance, more than 260 civilians had been killed by landmines along the so-called contact line. In 2017, the SMM medic Joseph Stone was killed while on patrol "when an SMM armored vehicle was struck by an explosion, most likely caused by an anti-tank mine in a non-government-controlled area near Pryshyb in the Luhansk region".[7]

After this incident, the SMM began to further limit its already constrained patrolling along the contact line to asphalted streets. Since the start of armed hostilities, the dilemma for the SMM's management team has been to try to strike a balance between maximum access and forward-

---

[5] "Factsheet: What is the OSCE?", *OSCE*, 19 September 2019, https://www.osce.org/whatistheosce/factsheet (accessed 4 April 2020).

[6] H. Katrine Haug, "The Minsk Agreements and the OSCE Special Monitoring Mission: Providing Effective Monitoring for the Ceasefire Regime", *Security and Human Rights*, vol. 27, nos. 3-4 (2016): 343. Also quoted in A. Härtel, A. Pisarenko and A. Umland, "The OSCE's Special Monitoring Mission to Ukraine: The SMM's Work in the Donbas and Its Ukrainian Critique in 2014–2019", *Security and Human Rights*, vol. 32 (2021), forthcoming. This article is partly reproduced here and lists most of the previously published analytical as well as some first academic papers on the SMM, in its footnotes.

[7] "OSCE SMM Chief Monitor Çevik pays tribute to SMM medic who died in the cause of peace", *OSCE*, 23 April 2020, https://www.osce.org/special-monitoring-mission-to-ukraine/450589 (accessed 2 May 2021).

leaning operations, on the one hand, and full security for its monitors on the ground, on the other. Russia obviously wants a constrained and tame Mission that operates and reports in a way that fits—or at least does not undermine—its "civil war" narrative on the Donbas conflict.[8]

The SMM is thus only partly comparable to some former operations in the Western Balkans, such as the OSCE Kosovo Verification Mission or the OSCE Task Force for Kosovo. Together with the OSCE Project Coordinator in Ukraine and the OSCE Observer Mission at the Russian Federation checkpoints Gukovo and Donetsk,[9] the SMM in Ukraine constitutes an especially heavy presence of the OSCE in an active conflict location. It is, moreover, monitoring a currently low-intensity and delegated, but still frightening, interstate war between Europe's territorially two largest states.[10]

Russia, moreover, has the world's largest arsenal of nuclear warheads while Ukraine no longer has any nuclear weapons. Ukraine had for a short period in the early 1990s been the world's third largest nuclear-weapon state. Under pressure from both Washington and Moscow, Kyiv gave up its entire atomic arsenal in exchange for explicit security assurances provided at a Conference on Security and Cooperation in Europe summit in Budapest in December 1994 (when the CSCE was renamed into OSCE). These assurances were provided by the three depositary states of the 1968 Treaty on the Non-Proliferation of Nuclear Weapons (Non-Proliferation Treaty, NPT)—the Russian Federation, the United

---

8   J. Hauter, ed., *Civil War? Interstate War? Hybrid War? Dimensions and Interpretations of the Donbas Conflict in 2014-2020* (Stuttgart: *ibidem*-Verlag, 2021).
9   Donetsk is a Russian town on the border with Ukraine and should not be confused with the Ukrainian Donbas city of the same name, which is the capital of Donets'ka oblast'. The OSCE monitors are, in Russia's Donetsk, observing Russian-Ukrainian border traffic at one checkpoint (and in Gukovo at another one).
10  J. Hauter, "Delegated Interstate War: Introducing an Addition to Armed Conflict Typologies", *Journal of Strategic Security*, vol. 12, no. 4 (2019): 90-103.

Kingdom and United States—as well as, in separate statements, by the two other official nuclear-weapon states under the NPT, China and France.[11] Finally, it is sometimes forgotten that Ukraine is home to Europe's largest nuclear power plant, in the south-eastern Zaporishshs'ka oblast', approximately 250 km from the current combat zone.

The Mission is part and parcel of the OSCE's role as an intermediary between Kyiv and Moscow in what in Ukraine is often called the Minsk process—a phrase that is actually reserved in internal OSCE parlance for another negotiation format concerning Nagorno-Karabakh. The Donbas-related Minsk format began in the early autumn of 2014 and brings together Ukraine, Russia and the OSCE in the above-mentioned TCG. The SMM Chief Monitor is also the moderator/coordinator of the TCG Working Group on Security Issues.

The TCG meetings are conducted in the semi-official presence of representatives of what are termed "certain areas of the Donets'k Oblast'" (CADO) and "certain areas of the Luhans'k Oblast" (CALO), or, as the Moscow-controlled pseudo-states label themselves and are known in Russia, the "Donetsk People's Republic" and the "Lugansk People's Republic" (DNR/LNR).

The negotiations are based on Minsk-1 (the Minsk Protocol) and Minsk-2 (the "Package of Measures"), two agreements signed by Ukraine's representative, former President Leonid Kuchma; Russia's representative, then Ambassador to Ukraine Mikhail Zurabov; and Ambassador Heidi Tagliavini of Switzerland on 5 September 2014 and 12 February 2015, respectively. However, the Minsk-2 Package of

---

11 M. Budjeryn and A. Umland, "Damage Control: The Breach of the Budapest Memorandum and the Nuclear Non-Proliferation Regime", in *NATO's Enlargement and Russia: A Strategic Challenge in the Past and Future*, edited by Oxana Schmies (Stuttgart: *ibidem*-Verlag, 2021), 177-189.

Measures was de facto negotiated by the presidents of Ukraine, Russia and France, as well as by Germany's Federal Chancellor within what became known as the Normandy Format.

Although the Normandy Four meetings were independent and had no formal mandate to task the OSCE, the documents emanating from them—somewhat paradoxically—mention the OSCE prominently. The second and fourth points of the Minsk Protocol assign the OSCE the task of monitoring the ceasefire and the Russian-Ukrainian border.[12] Minsk-2 mentions the OSCE in its second, third and tenth points, in connection with the issues of monitoring the withdrawal of heavy weapons from, a ceasefire in and the demilitarization of the conflict zone.[13] The arcane terminology that has evolved for diplomatic communications on the conflict, as well as the legally ambivalent status of the Minsk accords and Normandy Four in relation to the OSCE, can be seen as illustrations that for the Kremlin, these negotiations, their peculiar format and documents—including their definitions of the parties to the Donbas conflict—are part and parcel of Russia's hybrid aggression against Ukraine.[14]

---

12 "Protokol po itogam Trekhstoronnei kontaktnoi gruppy otnositel'no sovmestnykh shagov, napravlennykh na implementatsiiu Mirnogo plana Prezidenta Ukrainy Poroshenko i initsiativ Prezidenta Rossii V. Putina", *OSCE*, 5 September 2014, https://www.osce.org/files/f/documents/a/a/123258.pdf (accessed 5 October 2020).

13 "Kompleks mer po vypolneniiu Minskikh soglashenii", *OSCE*, 12 February 2015, https://www.osce.org/ru/cio/140221 (accessed 5 October 2019).

14 A. Umland, "Why the EU Should Decouple Sanctions Against Russia from the Minsk Agreements", *Harvard International Review*, 15 July 2016, www.academia. edu/27014352/Why_the_EU_Should_Decouple_Sanctions_Against_Russia_fr om_the_Minsk_Agreements (accessed 21 May 2021); M. Galeotti, "The Minsk Accords: Should Britain Declare Them Dead?", *Britain's World*, 24 May 2021, www.geostrategy.org.uk/britains-world/the-minsk-accords-should-britain-d eclare-them-dead/ (accessed 21 May 2021).

## Challenges to and Discussions of the SMM's Mandate

The nature, competencies and reach of the OSCE SMM to Ukraine have been at the centre of a seven-year long contestation. The monitoring mandate—unchanged since 2014— formally covers the entire territory of Ukraine. However, since Russia no longer considers the Crimea peninsula to be Ukrainian territory, Moscow made it clear from the start of the Mission that the SMM will not be given access to Crimea. The OSCE's original decision to establish the SMM was accompanied by an "Interpretative Statement" by Moscow that violated some of the basic principles of the Organization— the territorial integrity and the political sovereignty of participating states:

> In joining the consensus regarding the draft decision of the Permanent Council on the deployment of an OSCE Special Monitoring Mission to Ukraine, the Russian Federation proceeds from the assumption that the geographical area of deployment and activities of the mission in question is strictly limited by the parameters of the mandate as adopted today, which reflects the political and legal realities existing since 21 March 2014 as a result of the fact that the Republic of Crimea and Sevastopol have become an integral part of the Russian Federation.[15]

In response, Ukraine, the United States and Canada published their own official Interpretive Statements, remarking that Crimea is Ukrainian territory and that the SMM should therefore have access to the peninsula.[16] The European Union (EU) issued no such additional note, a notable European failure that was apparently due to a lack of agreement on the issue among the EU member states.

---

15 Organization for Security and Co-operation in Europe Permanent Council, "Decision No. 1117: Deployment of an OSCE Special Monitoring Mission to Ukraine", *OSCE*, 21 March 2014, https://www.osce.org/files/f/documents/d/6/116747.pdf (accessed 15 May 2021).
16 Ibid.

The Mission therefore has a significant presence, with hubs and forward patrol bases, only on Ukraine's mainland (in the Donbas there were 578 monitors in the spring of 2021) and to a lesser extent in Kyiv, where it has a head office, and the cities of Chernivtsi, Dnipro, Ivano-Frankivs'k, Kharkiv, Kherson, L'viv, and Odesa (187 monitors as of the spring of 2021). In this connection, the SMM has been occasionally also asked to observe situations unrelated to the Russian-Ukrainian conflict. In late 2020, for instance, Hungary publicly demanded the involvement of the SMM in the monitoring of a tense situation in some settlements of the Hungarian minority in western Ukraine's Transcarpathian region.[17] With its strident rhetoric and largely unfounded accusations against Kyiv, Budapest has been implicitly supporting the official Russian narrative that ethnic tensions within Ukraine and the nationalist policies of Kyiv have led to an allegedly "civil" war in the Donbas.

The major problem of the SMM, however, is that, in spite of its mandate and clear task to monitor the entire Donbas conflict zone, the SMM still has incomplete access to large parts of the CADO/CALO. In an April 2021 report, the OSCE complained about the limitations on the movement of the SMM:

> Almost all restrictions (93 per cent) occurred in non-government-controlled areas [i.e. the occupied and de facto Moscow-ruled territories of Ukraine's eastern Donets' Basin]. Half of the restrictions were recorded at checkpoints of the armed formations along official crossing routes on the contact line, preventing the SMM from crossing it during patrolling. The Mission was

---

17  S. Liechtenstein, "'Outrageous and Unacceptable': Hungarian Foreign Minister on the Situation in the Transcarpathian Region", *Security and Human Rights Monitor*, 4 December 2020, www.shrmonitor.org/outrageous-and-unacceptable-hungarian-foreign-minister-complains-about-situation-in-ukrainian-region-at-osce-ministerial-meeting/ (accessed 27 May 2021); "Statement by the Delegation of Ukraine in Response to the Current Issue Raised by the Delegation of Hungary", *OSCE*, 29 December 2020, www.osce.org/files/f/documents/6/f/476461.pdf (accessed 27 May 2021).

also prevented from moving between non-government-controlled areas of Donets'k and Luhans'k regions almost entirely. The SMM's monitoring of border areas beyond government control continued to be systematically limited due to restrictions to the Mission's access both in the areas and on the routes leading towards them. As a consequence, the Mission's observations in such border areas could again not be fully categorized as comprehensive and independent monitoring. [...] SMM unmanned aerial vehicles (UAV) continued to be subjected to GPS signal interference and gunfire, which limited the SMM's monitoring and put Mission members and technological assets at risk. Despite repeated requests by the Mission and the raising of the issue by the OSCE Chairperson-in-Office and the SMM Chief Monitor at the OSCE Permanent Council (PC), these restrictions were not eased and problems remained throughout the entire reporting period. Failure to remove mines, unexploded ordnance (UXO) and other explosive objects, and the laying of new ones, also continued to restrict the Mission's freedom of movement. Furthermore, the SMM also continued to face impediments in establishing and reporting facts following specific incidents and reports of incidents in non-government-controlled areas.[18]

The SMM remains a purely civilian mission that monitors the conflict but cannot intervene, at least, not on the spot, as this would require a peacekeeping or -enforcing mandate. The SMM plays a dialogue facilitation role on the ground, while initiating and supporting, for instance, localized ceasefires to allow the repair of critical civilian infrastructure, humanitarian operations and demining.[19] This modus operandi has been preserved even though Western analysts were already arguing in 2016 that—particularly during periods of conflict escalation—the SMM's purely "civil mandate is not adequate for such a tense and violent situation".[20]

Such ideas, however, not only encounter resistance from Russia and its allies among the OSCE states, but also come up against the fundamental challenge that the OSCE has no

---

18 *Thematic Report: Restrictions to the SMM's Freedom of Movement and Other Impediments to the Fulfilment of Its Mandate, July-December 2020* (Kyiv: OSCE SMM, 2021), i-ii.
19 S. Tolstov, "Diial'nist' mizhnarodnyh organizatsiy v Ukraini: zahal'ni tendentsii ta orientyry", *Viche*, no. 4 (2015): 11-15.
20 K. Hrant and S. Meister, "Ukraine, Russia and the EU: Breaking the Deadlock in the Minsk Process", *CEPS Working Document*, no. 423 (2016): 3, https://biblio.ugent.be/publication/8514008 (accessed 1 October 2019).

experience of the deployment of armed missions to a participating state, let alone one still facing an active conflict.[21] A 2016 suggestion by then President of Ukraine Petro Poroshenko that the SMM should be armed was resolutely rejected by all the other relevant actors, among other things because that would expose the, thus far, unarmed civilian monitors to new threats.[22]

In addition, further continuing limitations on the Mission's current and future mandate are linked to funding issues. The SMM's budget is not part of the OSCE Unified Budget,[23] but linked to and defined by its specific mandate in the Donbas.[24]

At various stages of the conflict, alongside discussions of a fundamental transformation of the SMM's mandate, peace operations by other organizations — notably the UN — have also been discussed (see below).[25] An EU police force for Ukraine was also suggested, even though neither of the parties to the Donbas conflict is a member of the EU.[26] The

---

21 The only case where the OSCE has mandated an armed mission regards Nagorno-Karabakh in a future situation to oversee a peace deal. Yet, this operation has never happened and may never happen as the OSCE Minsk Group was sidelined by Russia and Turkey in autumn 2020.
22 K. Bosko, "Die Debatte um eine bewaffnete OSZE-Mission in der Ostukraine", *Ukraine-Analysen*, no. 171 (2016): 19-20.
23 "Permanent Council Decision No. 1326", OSCE, 11 April 2019, https://www.osce.org/permanent-council/417164 (accessed 5 October 2019).
24 "Permanent Council Decision No. 1323", OSCE, 29 March 2019, https://www.osce.org/permanent-council/415988 (accessed 5 October 2019).
25 The earliest such suggestions were: A. Novak, "What's Peace in the Donbas Worth to Us? Why the International Community Should Propose a UN Protectorate", *Osteuropa-Plattform der Grünen*, 4 December 2014, grueneosteuropaplattform.wordpress.com/2014/12/04/whats-peace-in-the-donbas-worth-to-us-by-andrej-novak/ (accessed 1 October 2019); V. Kravchenko, "'Blakytni kasky' u donets'komu stepu", *Dzerkalo tyzhnia*, 20 February 2015, https://dt.ua/internal/blakitni-kaski-u-doneckomu-stepu-_.html (accessed 1 October 2019).
26 On the first such proposal: S. Blockmans and D. Gros, "The Case for EU Police Mission Ukraine", *CEPS*, 14 May 2014, https://www.ceps.eu/ceps-publications/case-eu-police-mission-ukraine/ (accessed 1 October 2019). See also: O. Melnyk and A. Umland, "Beyond the Minsk Agreements: Why and How a Combined UN/EU Peacekeeping Mission Could Disentangle the Donbas

supposition behind most of these proposals was, and still is, that a supplementary mission (or several combined missions) would complement the current purely civilian efforts of the SMM through additional—above all military—means. However, these debates, so far, remain hypothetical. Western countries have not yet been ready to send troops to Ukraine while Russia opposes this within the UN Security Council. At one point a proposal was circulated, by Russia, for a very small UN operation in Ukraine, but this was not a sufficiently robust armed mission that could have changed the status quo in the occupied territories, and was thus rejected by Ukraine as well as the West.[27]

## Successes and Hindrances of the SMM's Activities

Perhaps the most important accomplishment of the SMM so far is its longevity on the spot. The mere physical presence— "to see and be seen"—of international observers since the very early days of the conflict has raised the threshold for further armed conflict. It has most probably prevented escalations and atrocities that might have happened without the SMM in place. The SMM functions as a kind of thermometer of the conflict. If it were forced out of the CADO/CALO or became more restricted in its operation, this would constitute early warning of coming violence.

The SMM daily reports provide a considerable amount of data that, with each passing year, becomes more conclusive. The constantly growing number of observations allows

---

Conundrum", *European Council on Foreign Relations*, 30 March 2016, www.ecfr.eu/article/commentary_beyond_the_minsk_agreements (accessed 5 October 2019).

27 A. Umland, "UN Peacekeeping in Donbas? The Stakes of the Russia-Ukraine Conflict", *European Council on Foreign Relations*, 8 June 2018. ecfr.eu/article/commentary_un_peacekeeping_in_donbas_the_stakes_of_the_russia_ukraine_confl/ (accessed 5 October 2019).

for synchronic and diachronic comparison, statistical analysis and historic interpretation. For example, the SMM recorded 312,554 ceasefire violations in 2018, a number that was almost 25% lower than it was in 2017 but largely similar to the number of such violations recorded in 2016.[28]

Despite the relatively impressive scale of the SMM, it is too small and, as indicated above, too restricted in its mobility to adequately cover the more than 17,000 square kilometres of the conflict zone.[29] The SMM monitoring and reporting methodology also has limitations. For instance, the observations follow certain patrolling algorithms that are perhaps partly known to the combatants rather than the dynamics of the ceasefire violations. One shot — even if fired during an exercise rather than a skirmish — may be counted as a violation in the same way as far more serious hostile artillery fire would be. If several monitors and/or sensors hear or see the same bullet or warhead, each observation could be counted as a separate incident and thus reported as allegedly constituting several ceasefire violations. In short, to rely solely on the SMM's reporting for a depiction of reality can be misleading.

That said, the effectiveness of the SMM's observation activity over the years has greatly improved as a result of increasingly sophisticated monitoring methodology and technology. A 2021 report by the SMM on developments in the second half of 2020 notes that:

---

28  "Trends and observations from the Special Monitoring Mission to Ukraine", *OSCE*, https://www.osce.org/special-monitoring-mission-to-ukraine/417620 (accessed 2 October 2019) as quoted in Härtel, Pisarenko and Umland, "The OSCE's Special Monitoring Mission to Ukraine".
29  A. Safarov, "Novyi plan shchodo Donbasu: OON ta OBSE vidpovidaiut' za bezpeku, ES—za vidbudovu", *Deutsche Welle*, 29 January 2019, https://www.dw.com/uk/новий-план-щодо-донбасу-оон-та-обсє-відповідають-за-безп еку-єс-за-відбудову/a-47276080 (accessed 1 October 2019).

> The SMM continued to operate 27 cameras—deployed to 23 locations—19 in government-controlled areas, four in non-government-controlled areas and four between government- and non-government-controlled areas. The lower number of SMM cameras in non-government-controlled areas is a consequence of the refusal of those in control of these areas to offer the necessary support and assistance for the installation of cameras. […] The SMM's ability to monitor the areas near the international border continued also to be affected by the ongoing failure of those in control in non-government-controlled areas to offer the necessary security assurances to open forward patrol bases (FPBs) in settlements in the vicinity of border areas outside of government control.[30]

Another fundamental oddity of the Mission is that Russian citizens, as citizens of an OSCE participating state, are part of the staff on a permanent basis, in spite of the fact that the Kremlin was the original instigator of and continues to drive the conflict.[31] Some of the Russian monitors are suspected of espionage.[32]

The OSCE Observer Mission at the Russian Checkpoints Gukovo and Donetsk (but not Donets'k) is separate from the main OSCE mission and represents yet another peculiar facet of the overall monitoring efforts by the OSCE in the Donbas.[33] In contrast to these two small border locations, the Russia-led separatists deny permanent direct access to other parts of the Russian-Ukrainian border, where their irregular forces control the Ukrainian side. The area of the OSCE Mission at the two Russian checkpoints covers just 40 metres, of a 409-km

---

30   *Thematic Report*, 12 & 9.
31   "More Russians among OSCE observers in Donbas. Manipulations detected in reports", *InformNapalm*, 9 January 2020, informnapalm.org/en/more-russians-among-osce-observers-in-donbas/ (accessed 9 January 2020).
32   A. Quinn, "Russian OSCE monitor in Ukraine fired after drunkenly saying he was a Moscow spy", *The Telegraph*, 30 October 2015, https://www.telegraph.co.uk/news/worldnews/europe/russia/11965191/Russian-OSCE-monitor-in-Ukraine-fired-after-drunkenly-saying-he-was-a-Moscow-spy.html (accessed 1 October 2019).
33   O. Snihyr, "Rosiys'kyy ekspansionizm u Moldovi, Hruzii ta Ukraini: paraleli ta vidminnosti", *Dzerkalo Tyzhnia*, 19 May 2018, https://dt.ua/internati onal/rosiyskiy-ekspansionizm-u-moldovi-gruziyi-ta-ukrayini-paraleli-y-vid minnosti-278236_.html (accessed 1 October 2019).

border that is currently not under the control of Ukraine (i.e. the section between the separatist so-called people's republics and Russia).[34] The SMM 's official mandate "task[s] observers, operating under the principles of impartiality and transparency, with monitoring and reporting on the situation at the checkpoints of Donetsk and Gukovo, as well as on the movements across the border".[35] The monitors on the spot, however, are not even allowed to move around freely on the territory of the very checkpoints they are supposed to observe. The partly irrelevant reports from this separate and circumscribed second OSCE mission in the war zone are used by the Kremlin to support Russia's claims of non-involvement in the conflict.

The main function of this separate border mission is to provide Moscow with a fig leaf argument that the Russian-Ukrainian state border is being monitored. The OSCE Mission at Gukovo and Donetsk is designed to distract rather than to inform the public, and to conceal rather than to document what is going on between the CADO/CALO, on one side, and Russia, on the other. What is really needed is comprehensive monitoring of the entire perimeter currently not controlled by Ukraine's government. This would, however, demand a significant increase in SMM staff and resources to enable the SMM to provide continuous on-the-ground monitoring of this 409-km section of border.[36]

---

34  Y. Filipenko, "Statement in response to Ambassador Gyorgy Varga, Chief Observer of the OSCE Observer Mission at two Russian checkpoints on the Russian-Ukrainian border", *Ministry of Foreign Affairs of Ukraine*, 15 February 2018, mfa.gov.ua/en/news/62982-statement-in-response-to-ambassador-gyorgy-vargachief-observer-of-the-osce-observer-missionat-two-russian-checkpoints-on-the-russian-ukrainian-border (accessed 25 May 2021).
35  "Permanent Council Decision No. 1130", *OSCE*, 25 July 2014, www.osce.org/pc/121826 (accessed 1 October 2019).
36  T. Sylina, "Mins'ka khalabuda", *Dzerkalo tyzhnia*, 28 August 2015, https://dt.ua/internal/minska-halabuda-_.html (accessed 1 October 2019).

One recurring problem of the SMM's movements in the non-government-controlled area in earlier periods was that the monitors were threatened or attacked while conducting their patrols.[37] In some cases, OSCE monitors were arrested and held by pro-Russian warlords. Sometimes, their cars were fired at.[38] Parked vehicles and monitoring equipment were deliberately destroyed.[39] In recent years, OSCE SMM long-range cameras have frequently been destroyed, turned off or prevented from being installed by Russia-led separatists.[40] UAVs have been jammed and shot at.

All this in spite of the fact all the signatories to the Minsk Protocol agreed to "ensure permanent monitoring on the Ukrainian-Russian state border and verification by the OSCE, together with the creation of a safety zone in the border regions of Ukraine and the Russian Federation".[41] In April 2021, OSCE Secretary General Helga Schmid declared: "I am deeply concerned by recent incidents affecting the SMM, notably heavy interference with its technical assets and persistent freedom of movement restrictions. The SMM's safe and secure access throughout Ukraine is more important than

---

37  I. Ievtushenko, "The role and place of international organizations in the settlement of armed conflicts in the southeast of Ukraine (legal aspects)", *Problems of Legality*, no. 131 (2015): 124-132.
38  "OSCE Special Monitoring Mission patrol comes under fire in Donbas", *Censor.net*, 10 June 2019, https://censor.net.ua/en/news/3131451/osce_special_monitoring_mission_patrol_comes_under_fire_in_donbas (accessed 1 October 2019).
39  V. Kotyhorenko, "Chy mozhlyve zhyttia poza Mins'kom?" *Dzerkalo tyzhnia*, 24 June 2016, https://dt.ua/internal/chi-mozhlive-zhittya-poza-minskom-_.html (accessed 1 October 2019).
40  "Neshchodavno vstanovlenu na skhodi Ukrainy kameru SMM OBSE znyshcheno vohnem zi strilets'koi zbroi", *OSCE*, 10 August 2017, https://www.osce.org/uk/special-monitoring-mission-to-ukraine/335281 (accessed 5 October 2019); "Boiovyky 'DNR' vidkliuchyly kamery OBSE v raiyoni Donets'koho aeroportu", *Ukrinform*, 23 May 2016, https://www.ukrinform.ua/rubric-ato/2021679-bojoviki-dnr-vidklucili-kameri-obse-v-rajoni-doneckogo-aeroportu.html (accessed 1 October 2019).
41  "Protokol", point 4.

ever in the current circumstances of heightened tensions in the region".⁴²

The OSCE is an intergovernmental organization that makes its decisions by consensus, which means that the Sword of Damocles of a veto by Russia and its allies always looms large. This constrains and even shapes the political agenda, daily behavior and external communications of the Organization and its sub-units. Such defects become especially dysfunctional when it is necessary, as in the case of Russia's role in Transnistria, South Ossetia or the Donbas, to clearly and officially identify a party to a "hybrid" conflict that is a member of the OSCE.⁴³ Not only Moscow-controlled and equipped paramilitary units, but also Russia's regular army have been active in the CADO/CALO and large amounts of weapons have crossed the Russian-Ukrainian border, but none of this has ever been *explicitly* pointed out in the SMM's reporting.

As the Ukraine expert, Olena Snyhir, among others, has pointed out: "[t]he OSCE has the legal instrument to remove the aggressor state from its conflict resolution activities — a 'consensus minus one' principle that was adopted at the Prague OSCE Council of Ministers in 1992 and employed only once in relation to former Yugoslavia".⁴⁴ Thus far, however, the OSCE has not been willing or able to use this mechanism

---

42 As quoted in "OSCE Chairperson-in-Office Linde and Secretary General Schmid discussed recent developments in and around Ukraine", *OSCE*, 18 April 2021, www.osce.org/chairmanship/483818 (accessed 5 May 2021).
43 U. Schneckener, "Hybrider Krieg in Zeiten der Geopolitik? Zur Deutung und Charakterisierung des Donbass-Konflikts", *Politische Vierteljahresschrift*, vol. 57, no. 4 (2016): 586-613.
44 O. Snihyr, "OBSE v Ukraini: rol' Rosii, SMM ta pytannia myrotvorchoho kontyngentu", *Ukrains'ka pryzma*, 4 October 2016, http://prismua.org/osce-ukraine-role-russia-smm-peacekeepers/ (accessed 1 October 2019), as quoted in Härtel, Pisarenko and Umland, "The OSCE's Special Monitoring Mission to Ukraine".

with regard to Russia's deliberate circumscription of the SMM's overall role, concrete mandate, size and operation.

## Policy Recommendations on the SMM and Conflict Management

In spite of Russian resistance, Western policymakers and diplomats should attempt to improve the scope and efficiency of the SMM's framework and operation in the following ways:

*1. Organizational set-up:* The SMM should be given as much autonomy, freedom and leeway as possible within the OSCE with regard to its internal conduct, operation on the spot, public performance and official reporting. At the same time, the SMM's separate budget should be integrated into the OSCE's general budget to secure its connection to the Organization and continued operation for as long as necessary. The SMM should cooperate more closely and ideally be unified with the OSCE's separate mission at Gukovo and Donetsk. Because of the especially high demands of the SMM, staff recruited to it should be required to have previous operational experience in other missions. Some SMM staff should have relevant civilian and not only military or police experience in order to improve social patrolling and comprehensive reporting by the entire Mission. Inept staff members should be swiftly replaced without politicization by the sending participating state. The gender balance could be improved among senior managers and in certain other personnel categories. This would, among other things, enhance diversity and facilitate more effective social patrolling.

*2. Modalities of observation:* Western politicians and diplomats should put pressure on Russia to allow the SMM full, permanent, unhindered and round-the-clock freedom of movement and access to all parts of the conflict zone, especially on the Russian-Ukrainian border and ideally to Crimea.

More emphasis should be put on reporting and highlighting the presence of military equipment on Ukraine's territory that is not in the Ukrainian armed forces' inventory (i.e. Russian-supplied weapons). In view of the recent build-up of the Russian military presence in the Black Sea, the SMM may want to increase its presence in mainland southern Ukraine, especially by the Azov Sea and Isthmus of Perekop. At the same time, the SMM should be shielded from engaging in non-core activities, such as monitoring the situation of the Hungarian minority in western Ukraine. The OSCE member states and the EU should continue to provide sufficient funding for the SMM to operate. The Mission's budget should be further increased in order to: (a) enlarge the number of monitors and other staff; (b) improve the SMM's current technical equipment, including UAVs and cameras; and (c) obtain new equipment such as artillery sensors and radar systems. The SMM's monitors should, to the extent possible, investigate and report military fatalities in addition to civilian casualties. At the same time, the Mission's monitors should more fully engage in observation and description of important humanitarian issues, especially in the non-government controlled areas, linked not least to the grave human rights violations in the two pseudo-republics' notorious detention systems and torture prisons.[45]

3. *Content and style of reporting*: Reporting from the SMM should be (a) more reflective of the monitors' recorded

---

45  S. Aseyev and A. Umland, "'Isolation': Donetsk's Torture Prison", *Harvard International Review*, 4 December 2020, hir.harvard.edu/donetsks-isolation-torture-prison/ (accessed 2 May 2021); H. Coynash, "Human Rights Violations in the Occupied Parts of Ukraine's Donbas since 2014", *UI Reports on Human Rights and Security in Eastern Europe*, no. 1 (2021), https://www.ui.se/globalassets/butiken/ui-report/ui-report-no.-1-2021.pdf (accessed 2 May 2021); S. Aseyev and A. Umland, "Prisoners as Political Commodities in the Occupied Areas of the Donbas", *UI Reports on Human Rights and Security in Eastern Europe*, no. 2 (2021), www.ui.se/globalassets/ui.se-eng/publications/ui-publications/2021/ui-report-no-2-2021.pdf (accessed 2 May 2021).

observations on the spot (for example, the absence of unequivocal evidence for certain violations is often not evidence of an absence of such violations); (b) clearer and more transparent in terms of the political meaning of reported facts; and (c) more analytical and interpretative in its presentation. The filtering, redacting and coding of the information that flows from the monitors into the published reports should be reduced to a technical minimum. The political censorship and self-censorship linked to the consensus-based nature of organizations such as the OSCE need as far as possible to be avoided. As much as possible (in the light of various security and privacy considerations) of the large amount of raw oral, verbal, numerical, visual and audial data collected by the SMM—especially the imagery from UAVs and satellites—should be made openly accessible to the public sooner rather than later. The current daily reporting format may not be necessary during times of low-intensity conflict, when approximately three—analytical rather than merely factual—reports per week from the SMM may be sufficient. The SMM's current internal weekly reports should be made public immediately while a biweekly or monthly working paper series could publish scholarly and narrowly focused analyses of certain SMM-recorded events and developments by qualified internal or external experts. A future special reporting system for mainland southern Ukraine, in case of an escalation there, should perhaps already be being contemplated. The Mission's direct interaction with governmental institutions, interested media outlets, specialized think tanks, relevant NGOs and other international bodies, and individual academic researchers should be intensified in order to improve the verification, circulation and interpretation of the vast amount of information collected by the SMM.

4. *Accompanying measures*: Discussion of a fundamental reformatting of the current Mission, such as an arming or a substantive extension, should be conducted cautiously so as not to endanger the continuing existence of the SMM as an OSCE operation for as long as the conflict exists. A qualitative upgrading of the current international engagement in the Donbas could be sought through other organizations and institutions.[46] This would concern, above all, additional autonomous OSCE institutions explicitly mandated to cooperate with the SMM, such as the Office for Democratic Institutions and Human Rights (ODIHR) Representative on Freedom of the Media (RFoM) and High Commissioner on National Minorities (HCNM). These structures could become more involved in the monitoring and reporting of violations of OSCE commitments in the non-government-controlled areas while also cooperating more closely with the SMM, the United Nations, the Council of Europe (CoE) and other actors in the international community. The EU could, within its now fully functioning Association Agreement with Ukraine, return to the spring of 2014 idea of an EU police mission to eastern Ukraine, although such an operation would probably only get access to government-controlled areas. Within the EU's Eastern Partnership program, or other Ukraine-related multilateral initiatives, a range of conflict-related initiatives might be possible to support the activities of the OSCE in Ukraine through, for instance, research and publication projects based on SMM reports.

---

46  Whether an attempt to fully re-establish the Joint Control and Coordination Commission, which consisted of Russian and Ukrainian military officers and existed between 2015 and 2017, would make sense is, in view of its ambiguous record as a bilateral organ and defunct initiative, contested. W. Kemp, "Moving from War to Peace in Ukraine: The Role of a Joint Military Commission", *Security and Human Rights Monitor*, 29 April 2020, www.shrmonitor.org/moving-from-war-to-peace-the-role-of-a-joint-military-commission/ (accessed 2 May 2021).

*5. Towards a conflict solution*: Ukraine and its Western partners should continue to raise the issue of a large classical UN-mandated, combined armed and civilian peacekeeping mission to the Donbas. The task of such an operation, in close cooperation with the Ukrainian state, the SMM, the ODIHR, ReoM, the HCNM and the CoE, would be to ensure Russian troop withdrawal and Ukraine's full control over its international border, as well as the necessary conditions for the eventual holding of legitimate parliamentary elections (within single-mandate districts), and regional as well as local elections in the currently non-government-controlled areas.[47] Western governments should already today be developing contingency plans for the deployment and funding of a full-scale and sufficiently armed UN mission as well as a temporary international civilian administration in eastern Ukraine, in the highly unlikely event that Russia agrees in the Security Council to such a solution to the Donbas conflict.[48]

*Dr. Andreas Umland is an Analyst of the Stockholm Centre for Eastern European Studies at the Swedish Institute of International Affairs, Associate Professor of Political Science at the Kyiv-Mohyla Academy, and editor of the book series "Soviet and Post-Soviet Politics and Society" published by ibidem Press.*

---

47  M. Georg Link, "Die Wahlbeobachter müssen auf die Krim", *Neue Zürcher Zeitung*, 19 May 2015, www.nzz.ch/meinung/debatte/standards-nicht-zum-halben-preis-1.18544519?reduced=true (accessed 20 May 2021).
48  C. Bildt, "Is Peace in Donbass Possible?" *European Council on Foreign Relations*, 12 October 2017, www.ecfr.eu/article/commentary_is_peace_in_donbas_possible (accessed 1 October 2019); Andreas Umland, "Re-Imagining and Solving the Donbas Conflict: A Four-Stage Plan for Western and Ukrainian Actors", *Foreign Policy Association*, 29 August 2018, foreignpolicyblogs.com/2018/08/29/re-imagining-and-solving-the-donbas-conflict-a-four-stage-plan-for-western-and-ukrainian-actors/ (accessed 1 October 2019).

# Russia's Instrumentalization of Conflict
# The Protracted Conflicts as Open Wounds for European Security

*John Zachau*

DOI: https://doi.org/10.24216/9783838216881_009

## Executive summary

*Thirty years after the break-up of the Soviet Union, the vision of a Europe whole, free and at peace is "unfinished business", not least since several countries in Eastern Europe are still struggling with protracted conflicts. These conflicts are not only, or even mainly, local or regional in nature. Instead, they constitute a systemic challenge to the European security order, with consequences beyond the region itself. Georgia, Moldova and especially Ukraine are suffering from the Kremlin's manifest desire to establish a sphere of influence. Moscow also wants to prevent the spread of democracy, human rights and the rule of law, and aims ultimately to renegotiate the normative European security order as defined in international law and OSCE principles and commitments. Russia's external aggression towards these countries is paired with increasingly harsh repression within Russia, as well as in the non-government-controlled areas of the three states where regular and irregular Russian armed forces are deployed without host nation consent. Russia's instrumentalisation of these conflicts should also be seen in the context of its antagonistic behaviour elsewhere, including towards the EU and NATO. In the light of these challenges, the democratic international community must stick together and clearly acknowledge that all states in the OSCE region have the right to sovereignty and territorial integrity, and to freely choose their security arrangements, including treaties of alliance, as well as the right to self-defence according to international law. It must also be acknowledged that security between states is linked to conditions within them, as per the OSCE comprehensive security concept. The democratic international community should do more to hold Russia accountable for its violations of international law and the European security order, including with regard to Crimea. If not, there is a risk that the ongoing violations will become permanent, that customary international law and OSCE principles and commitments will be eroded, and that further transgressions will take place. The overarching goal of conflict resolution efforts must be the restoration of respect for international law and for OSCE principles and commitments. The existing conflict resolution – or rather conflict-management or even conflict-conservation – formats and mechanisms should be evaluated according to these criteria. To reach its political goals, Moscow instrumentalises these formats, which become the main battlefields rather than platforms for conflict resolution. It is therefore important to avoid "destructive ambiguity" when engaging in these formats, and to be clear about who the conflicting parties are and where responsibility lies. The democratic international community should refrain from any attempt at a "grand bargain" with Moscow that implicitly or explicitly accepts spheres of influence and reduced sovereignty for some states. This would effectively undermine international law and the European security order, reward the Kremlin for its transgressions and be unlikely to bring sustainable stability.*

## Introduction

The dissolution of the Soviet Union was largely, but not exclusively, peaceful. In the years around the break-up, hostilities broke out in Azerbaijan and, to a lesser extent, also in Armenia, as well as in Georgia and Moldova. These soon turned into protracted conflicts with wider geopolitical dimensions. In different but significant degrees, the hostilities were rooted in inter-ethnic or inter-cultural tensions that had been contained but not fully resolved in the Soviet era, or had had their seeds sown by Soviet policies towards ethnic minorities, internal boundary lines and varying degrees of regional autonomy, among other factors. The historical background was especially salient in the violence between ethnic Armenians and Azeris, which soon developed into an armed conflict between Armenia and Azerbaijan.

In Georgia and Moldova, however, the conflicts were also driven and instrumentalized by Russian actors early on; they, like President Vladimir Putin, considered the collapse of the Soviet Union not as a liberation from oppression but as "the greatest geopolitical catastrophe of the century". These players did not want to recognize the newly independent states as fully sovereign but aimed to keep them in the Russian orbit. During the hostilities in Georgia and Moldova in the early 1990s, Russian/former-Soviet armed units provided active and probably decisive support to the insurrectionists in the so-called breakaway republics. This Russian support has since continued alongside direct Russian antagonistic conduct vis-à-vis the legitimate authorities in both states, in violation of their political sovereignty and territorial integrity. The Russian "toolbox" for this strategy builds on Soviet practices and includes the use of military and paramilitary forces in different forms: as "peacekeepers" following Moscow-brokered/-dictated ceasefire agreements; through "passportization", propaganda, economic punishment and other hybrid measures; and, sometimes, using incentives, "soft power" initiatives and attempts to co-opt local elites.

If this approach was not already clear before August 2008, Russia's military intervention in Georgia, its territorial expansion of the two non-government-controlled areas, its subsequent recognition of these areas as independent states, and the consolidation of its military presence there, showed the Kremlin's disregard for international law, OSCE principles and commitments, and other obligations, including the six-point-agreement negotiated by the then presidents of Russia and France, Dmitry Medvedev and Nicolas Sarkozy. These steps were followed in 2014 by an even more blatant transgression in the form of Russia's unprovoked military aggression against Ukraine, which also involved its illegal annexation of Crimea. This created yet another protracted conflict that, almost eight years later, is still far from resolution and, if anything, risks escalating.

In spite of all these obvious transgressions, Russia refuses to acknowledge its role as a party to any of the conflicts. Its growing external aggression is accompanied by increasingly harsh repression inside Russia, as well as in the areas abroad where Russian armed forces are deployed without host nation consent and where the European Court of Human Rights has concluded, in several cases, that Russia is in effective control. Russia's aggression must also be seen against the background of its hybrid threats and antagonistic behavior towards the EU and NATO, their member states, and other organizations and states.

### Russia's Policy Priorities

Over time, it has become evident that Russia instrumentalizes conflict—and also conflict resolution processes—to achieve political goals. The protracted conflicts in Eastern Europe are thus not only, or even principally, local or regional but constitute a systemic challenge to the European security order, with consequences beyond the region itself.

Judging by Russian rhetoric and actions, the Kremlin is seeking to establish and maintain a sphere of influence over its "near abroad" and to prevent additional states in Eastern

Europe from orienting towards the "West", and in particular from joining or substantially cooperating with NATO and/or the EU—including individual member states. Instead, these Eastern European states should be under Moscow's control and function as buffer states or a cordon sanitaire that allows forward-deployed Russian military assets and the possibility of some kind of (re-)integration with Russia.

This is the case in Ukraine, Georgia and Moldova, where Russia has resorted to military means to perpetuate or even initiate conflict and used its position on the UN Security Council and within the OSCE to block any efforts to achieve conflict resolution in line with international law and OSCE principles and commitments. It also applies to Armenia and Azerbaijan, where Russia is less directly involved in the conflict but uses it to pursue its own interests, among other things by acting unilaterally outside of the established OSCE conflict resolution process to secure an exclusive role as a "peacekeeping force".

Underlying the objective to establish such concentric spheres of influence is the desire to prevent the spread of democracy, human rights and the rule of law, which are seen as existential threats by the Kremlin's current occupants. This aspect is particularly strong in relation to Ukraine, Georgia and Moldova, which all aspire to EU membership (and, with the exception of Moldova, also NATO membership).

Taken together, Russia's objectives ultimately amount to a decades-long, consistent attempt to renegotiate the normative European security order. In essence, the Russian leadership wants explicit approval or at least de facto acceptance of a new security order, one where supposed buffer states are not fully sovereign and do not have the right to choose their own security arrangements, and where issues related to human rights, fundamental freedoms, democracy and the rule of law should no longer be considered matters of direct and legitimate concern to other states; that is, a new order in direct contradiction of key tenets of the jointly agreed OSCE principles and commitments.

Despite Russia's frequent accusations and "whataboutism", the "West" is not to be blamed for this precarious situation. The EU and NATO have not "expanded" eastwards, but independent states in Central and Eastern Europe have freely chosen to strive for membership. Membership prospects, accession negotiations, leading to eventual accession to the EU and membership in NATO, were only achieved after considerable lobbying in Western capitals by prospective members. The two organizations do not seek to establish spheres of influence, but stand up for the jointly agreed European security order. In addition, the EU, NATO and their individual member states are not violating international law by deploying soldiers in Ukraine, Georgia and Moldova against their wishes. Russia is.

## The Particular Importance of Ukraine

Russia's military aggression against Ukraine and its illegal annexation of Crimea must be considered the gravest violation of the post-World War II European security order. Its covert instigation and perpetuation of conflict on Ukrainian territory has, among other things, led to over 14,000 deaths, over 1.5 million internally displaced persons and particularly grave human rights violations in the non-government-controlled areas. In terms of access to political rights and civil liberties, eastern Donbas and Crimea currently rank among the worst in the world.

The conflict is not just a "crisis in and around Ukraine" (as the Russia-dictated consensus language within the OSCE suggests) but a larger, systemic and transnational "Russia crisis" that affects not only Ukraine, but European security, the European security order and the rules-based international order as a whole. Through its ongoing aggression, Russia is violating international law, OSCE principles and commitments, and additional bilateral and multilateral agreements, including the 1994 promise in the Budapest Memorandum to respect Ukraine's independence, sovereignty and existing borders in return for Kyiv handing over the nuclear weapons on its territory to Russia.

Clearly, Putin wants Ukraine and a new security order that either de jure or de facto acknowledges this. As former US National Security Advisor Zbigniew Brzezinski famously observed in 1994: "without Ukraine, Russia ceases to be an empire, but with Ukraine suborned and then subordinated, Russia automatically becomes an empire". To this revanchist "great power urge" in the Kremlin can be added its fear that a successful Ukraine would inspire Russians to demand democratic change at home.

While, through its aggression, Russia has managed to impede Ukraine's path to NATO and EU membership, it would be naive to think that it considers its goals achieved. On the contrary, increasingly strong and disturbing signals have recently come from Moscow that the status quo is unacceptable. These signals include the Russian military build-up near the border with Ukraine and in Crimea in the spring of 2021, and the subsequent publication of revisionist articles on Ukraine by Putin and former president Dmitry Medvedev, now deputy head of the Russian Security Council. In addition, the Kremlin has distanced itself even further from the jointly agreed OSCE principles and commitments by making not only Ukrainian NATO membership but even NATO military infrastructure in Ukraine a "red line" for Russia. Russia also absurdly accuses Kyiv of "trying to drag Moscow into the conflict in eastern Ukraine" — a conflict that Moscow instigated and of which it is the driving force — while refusing to engage in the Normandy format (and publishing confidential correspondence from Berlin and Paris). Russia also complains about legitimate arms deliveries to Kyiv and demands "legal, juridical guarantees" in the form of "concrete agreements that would rule out any further eastward expansion of NATO and the deployment of weapons systems posing a threat to us in close proximity to Russia's territory". In addition, it conducts unexplained military activities in and around Ukraine that look worryingly like preparations for increased Russian military action in the country. To this list can be added Russia's Foreign Intelligence Service (SVR) publicly comparing the situation in Ukraine to Georgia in the run-up to the 2008 war, and the head of the Russian Security Council, Nikolai Patrushev, warning that "millions of Ukrainians" might need to flee at any moment.

While the gun has been put on the table, so to speak, it is safe to assume that the Kremlin is keeping several options open and currently testing the reactions from Kyiv and Western capitals. The objectives of this strategic signaling are clear: Kyiv should be more acquiescent and the "West" should not act against Russia's interests in its perceived sphere of influence.

Possibly related events are taking place elsewhere, such as Russia's gas supply issues with Europe, the cynical luring of migrants to Belarus to help or push them into the EU, and resurfacing tensions in the Western Balkans. Inside Russia, the imprisonment of Novichok victim Aleksandr Navalny continues, organizations affiliated with him have been designated as "extremist", and moves are being made to close down Russia's most prominent human rights group, Memorial. Something worrying is definitely in the air and we may already be deeper into "the next European security crisis" than many realize, even if we may one day talk rather about different episodes in a longer "Soviet/Russia crisis". It may be impossible to fully control continuing developments, but they can at least be influenced.

## Policy Recommendations

1. The democratic international community – the EU, the US and like-minded allies and partners – must stick together and try to further improve its internal coordination and cooperation. It should clearly acknowledge that all states in the OSCE region have the right to sovereignty and territorial integrity, and to freely choose their own security arrangements, including treaties of alliance, as jointly agreed within the OSCE, as well as the right to self-defense according to international law, with due respect to international humanitarian law and international human rights law. Without strong US leadership and a US presence in Europe, European cohesion around policies based on these principles will probably be increasingly difficult to achieve.

2. The democratic international community should further acknowledge that security between states is clearly linked to conditions within them, as per the OSCE's comprehensive security concept. Internal repression and external aggression are thus two sides of the same coin, meaning that violations of civil and political rights within states increase the risk of violations of international law between states – and vice versa. In the OSCE region, the level of respect for democracy, the rule of law and human rights in one state is therefore a matter of direct and legitimate concern for other states. Among other things, UN, OSCE, EU and Council of Europe instruments should be directed at the particularly severe situation in those non-government-controlled areas

where the Russian military is overtly or covertly deployed without host nation consent. Nor should the increasing repression inside Russia be forgotten. It should be addressed head on, including through strengthened support for Russian civil society actors.

3. The democratic international community should do more to keep the various transgressions — including Crimea — on the international agenda and increase its focus on accountability. Failure to hold the main perpetrator in the region, Russia, accountable for all its blatant violations of international law and other constituent elements of the jointly agreed European security order would amount to tacit acceptance of a new de facto security order. This would not only risk making ongoing violations permanent, but also erode customary international law and OSCE principles and commitments, increasing the likelihood of further transgressions, even against EU and NATO member states — and elsewhere in the world.

4. The overarching goal of conflict resolution efforts must be the restoration of respect for international law and OSCE principles and commitments. Existing conflict resolution efforts — or rather conflict-management or even conflict-conservation formats and mechanisms — should be evaluated according to this criterion. To achieve its political goals, Moscow instrumentalizes these formats, which have now become the main battlefields of these conflicts rather than platforms for their resolution. It is therefore important to avoid "destructive ambiguity" when engaging in these formats and to be clear about who the conflicting parties are and where responsibility lies. Among other things, support for monitoring through OSCE, UN, EU or Council of Europe missions must continue and "business as usual" with Moscow must be resisted until ongoing violations have ceased. To achieve the

required change in behavior and to prevent further transgressions, sanctions should be considered, prepared, signaled, imposed, maintained or strengthened, as deemed appropriate on a case-by-case basis.

5. The democratic international community should refrain from appeasement and any attempts at an explicit or implicit "grand bargain" with Moscow over the heads of states already affected by or at risk of Russian aggression. A formal renegotiation or de facto acceptance of a new European security order that somehow, either implicitly or explicitly, acknowledges a Russian sphere of influence or forces "in-between status" on certain states would undermine their sovereignty and rights, and have consequences far beyond the region. It would also be contrary to the principle in international law of "no fruits from aggression", since the Kremlin would in effect be rewarded for its transgressions. Moreover, it would be unlikely to bring stability since the affected states (or parts of them) would not necessarily comply with any such "deal" or "compromise", and since democratic, open societies are seen by the Kremlin as threats not only because of what they do, but also for what they represent. Even in such a scenario, Russia's antagonistic behavior would therefore be very likely to continue, albeit from a new baseline and with a whetted appetite.

6. The democratic international community should acknowledge that defense of the normative European security order must be backed up by genuine investments in security and defense. While this is being pursued within NATO and at many national levels, more should be done to support the development of resilience and defense capabilities in the Eastern European states already affected by Russian aggression. Failure to do so would de facto amount to giving in to Russian threats. Even though many EU member states

perceive no immediate threat or feel any sense of urgency, Ukraine's defense against ongoing Russian aggression is also a defense of European security and of the European security order. Any submission by Ukraine to Russian pressure would also be a submission by the democratic international community—with implications beyond Ukraine.

7. The democratic international community should continue—and, if possible, strengthen—its assistance to Ukraine and other conflict-affected states in areas not directly related to the conflicts. Through support for democratic and economic development more generally, the states' resilience and ability to deal with the conflicts will increase, as will their attractiveness to the populations in the currently non-government-controlled areas and their function as role models for democratization elsewhere. A conditional "tough love" approach will probably be needed to deal with certain worrying trends in states such as Georgia and Ukraine. Efforts must also be stepped up to combat the laundering of monies and reputations in Western societies, regardless of their origin.

*John Zachau was, in 2021-2022, an Analyst of the Stockholm Centre for Eastern European Studies at the Swedish Institute of International Affairs. Since 2022, he is a Desk Officer at the Office of the Prime Minister of Sweden.*

# International Law and Accountability in Relation to the Protracted Conflicts in Eastern Europe*

*Marika Ericson and Isak Malm*

DOI: https://doi.org/10.24216/9783838216881_010

## Executive Summary

*International law draws a clear distinction between rules for peace and rules for war, but reality has not always corresponded to this clear distinction. In the case of the protracted conflicts in Eastern Europe, classic military use of force has been combined with other antagonistic measures. An additional complicating factor in relation to these protracted conflicts is the difficulty in identifying the parties, partly due to the use of proxies and covert operations, which in turn clouds which legal framework is applicable. This lack of clarity causes further issues in relation to accountability for violations of International Law. Nonetheless, International Law – including International Humanitarian Law (IHL) and International Human Rights Law – is applicable, subject to the facts on the ground, and provides various avenues for accountability. A fairly unsurprising finding is that if a permanent member of the UN Security Council commits acts that constitute a threat to international peace and security, the Security Council is unable to react due to the existence of the permanent members' veto. However, international – and to some extent national – courts can be used to hold an aggressive neighbour accountable for violations of International Law. In*

---

\* The authors are grateful for the valuable comments and input received while working on this report from Professor Jann Kleffner, Swedish Defence University. This article was written before Russia's renewed aggression against Ukraine on 24 February 2022, an event affecting further the international law dimensions applicable to the conflict.

relation to Ukraine, a number of judicial proceedings have been, and could potentially be, initiated in the European Court of Human Rights, the International Criminal Court, the International Court of Justice, the Permanent Court of Arbitration and the International Tribunal for the Law of the Sea. While these processes of accountability take time, and there are many hurdles that need to be overcome, such processes are ongoing and most will in time reach a conclusion.

## Introduction

When Russia began its military intervention in Crimea in 2014 and the situation in eastern Ukraine escalated, international law quickly became part of the debate. What kind of conflict or conflicts is Ukraine involved in? How can, or should, international law ensure accountability and mitigate further hostilities? Which legal forums are available to a state such as Ukraine to take legal action against an aggressive neighbor? A rather unsurprising lesson learned is that a permanent member of the United Nations Security Council, acting with aggression against another state, was able to forestall any effective response by the UN. Supranational organizations like the EU, and its individual member states, have imposed sanctions — but is that enough?

International law draws a clear distinction between rules for peace and rules for war. Peace is the state of normality where all regular rules apply in the relations between states. War, on the other hand, is the exception to the rule; in this case, special rules apply to the parties to the conflict, and in the relationships between other states and the parties to a conflict. Despite the fact that the law draws a clear distinction between peace and war, reality has never entirely corresponded to that clear distinction. The ongoing armed conflict situations involving Ukraine are a clear example of how modern conflicts combine other types of antagonistic measures alongside the classic military-type use of force or military operations.

Throughout history, states have often used the term "war" in a political setting, rather than as the legal category of an ongoing conflict.[1] States may have strategic and political reasons for not openly stating that they are parties to an ongoing armed conflict. Today, however, the legal frameworks are largely dependent on the facts on the ground rather than the subjective views of states. As is shown below, they are formulated in such a way that they apply regardless of how states categorize their ongoing dispute with another state.

In the case of the conflicts in Eastern Europe, multiple complicating features are highly conspicuous. The narratives framing, and the available information about, the conflicts are markedly different on the opposing sides, and some news outlets provide propaganda rather than news. The conflicts contain cyber-elements and disinformation, and there are clear elements of "lawfare", that is, to put it briefly, the use of law as a weapon of war.[2] In the case of Russia, this is visible, for instance, in its engagement in the debate in the UN about a global convention on cybercrime,[3] and also in its quite successful promotion of its narrative of the conflict in Ukraine. This, together with Russia's veto power in the UN Security Council, has made working for accountability difficult.[4]

---

1 For several examples see, e.g., C. Jessup, "*Intermediacy*", 23 Nordisk Tidsskrift Int'l Ret 16-26.
2 For a more in-depth definition and examples see, e.g., O. F. Kittrie, "*Lawfare*" (Oxford: Oxford University Press, 2016).
3 United Nations, General Assembly, "Countering the use of information and communications technologies for criminal purposes". A/RES/75/282, 26 May 2021.
4 S. D. Bachmann and A. B. Mosquera, "Lawfare and hybrid warfare: how Russia is using the law as a weapon", *Amicus Curiae: Journal of the Society for Advanced Legal Studies*, no. 102 (Summer 2015), updated 2016.

Several aspects are notable in relation to Ukraine and the other conflicts in Eastern Europe. In both the cyber and the physical domains, the use of proxies and of covert operations causes problems regarding accountability in accordance with International Law. Its use of such methods has been a standing accusation against Russia in the conflicts being played out in Georgia, Moldova and Ukraine.[5]

This paper begins by introducing International Law, International Human Rights Law and International Humanitarian Law (IHL), and specifically the applicability of IHL, which is also known as the law of armed conflict, in different situations—including in relation to the conflicts in Eastern Europe. Further, this paper discusses different avenues for establishing accountability for violations of International Law in conflict situations, including violations of IHL, and highlights how some of these avenues are being used in relation to Ukraine.

## International Law

International Law mainly regulates the relations between states, covering areas such as trade, diplomacy, the use of force and human rights. International Human Rights Law specifies the obligations states have to protect and respect the rights inherent to all human beings. Human Rights apply in times of both peace and armed conflict, but they can be limited to some extent during armed conflicts.

In armed conflicts, the *lex specialis* of IHL provides rules on the methods and means of warfare as well as rules to protect civilians and combatants. IHL has a long pedigree. Contemporary IHL is codified in a number of treaties, most

---

5   See, e.g., G. Lucas, "State-Sponsored Hacktivism and the Rise of 'Soft' War", in *"Soft War": The Ethics of Unarmed Conflict*, edited by M. L. Gross and T. Meisels (Cambridge: Cambridge University Press, 2017), 81ff.

notably the Four Geneva conventions of 1949 and their Additional Protocols of 1977 and 2005. In addition, Customary International Law is an important source of current IHL. Customary International Law is created when states, through general practice (*usus*) accepted as law (*opinio iuris*), create new rules that are applicable to all states.

## Different Types of Conflicts

Even though IHL is often discussed as a single cohesive framework, it distinguishes between International Armed Conflicts (IACs), which include belligerent occupation, and Non-International Armed Conflicts (NIACs). IACs are conflicts that are fought between two or more states,[6] while NIACs are fought between a state and an organized armed group or between two organized armed groups.[7] An IAC and an NIAC can exist in parallel; however, if a situation cannot be classified as either an IAC or an NIAC, IHL is inapplicable and the peacetime rules of International Law apply.

The distinction between IACs and NIACs is important for many reasons, not least because the Geneva conventions of 1949 only contain a single article that is applicable to NIAC: the third article of the conventions, often referred to as "Common Article 3". Common Article 3 establishes basic protection for those not participating in hostilities, for those who have put down their weapons and for those who are injured, sick or deprived of their liberty. Since the inception of

---

6 As regards the constitution of a state, the dominant view is that a state is defined as a person in international law. It has a permanent population, a defined territory, a government and the ability to enter into relations with the other states. See the Montevideo Convention on the Rights and Duties of States, 26 December 1933, article 1.
7 International Committee of the Red Cross (ICRC), Geneva Convention for the Amelioration of the Condition of the Wounded and Sick in Armed Forces in the Field (First Geneva Convention), 12 August 1949, 75 UNTS 31, art 2 and 3.

Common Article 3 in 1949, other IHL rules have evolved that also apply to NIACs, and there has been a certain degree of congruence between the law that applies to IACs and that which applies to NIACs.[8] Nevertheless, there remain key differences in the applicable law in the two types of conflict, such as *when* the law begins to apply,[9] as well as the rules regulating the treatment of prisoners of war,[10] and the law on belligerent occupation,[11] which is only applicable to IACs. Since the legal framework differs between the types of conflict, it is important from a legal perspective to identify the actors in an armed conflict. This not only establishes which rules apply to a given situation, but also helps to ensure accountability for acts that breach applicable rules. This can prove legally challenging, especially in instances where multiple armed conflicts occur in parallel, since different norms might be applicable to different actors.

From an International Law perspective, it is possible to argue that, in addition to the IAC between Ukraine and Russia linked to the occupation of Crimea, there are one or two NIACs between the government of Ukraine and the so-called Donetsk People's Republic and Lugansk People's Republic in eastern Ukraine. From a legal point of view, such conflicts are considered parallel to the IAC between Russia and Ukraine, and governed by a partly different legal framework. If it were possible to clearly establish that Russia was exerting overall

---

8   Importantly, the ICRC Customary International Humanitarian Law study has a list of 161 rules, 149 of which are applicable to NIACs. See J.-M. Henckaerts, "Study on customary international humanitarian law: A contribution to the understanding and respect for the rule of law in armed conflict", *International Review of the Red Cross*, vol. 87, no. 857 (2005): 198–212.
9   The Prosecutor v. Dusko Tadić, (IT-94-1-A), Decision on the Defence Motion for Interlocutory Appeal on Jurisdiction, 2 October 1995, para. 70.
10  S. Sivakumaran, *The Law of Non-international Armed Conflict* (Oxford: Oxford University Press, 2012), 521.
11  Ibid., 529.

control over rebel forces in this armed conflict, they would be reclassified as international in character.

In this context, it should be noted that the government of Ukraine considers the non-government-controlled parts of its territory to be occupied by Russia. Russia, for its part, claims that it is not a party to any international armed conflict with Ukraine.[12]

## International Armed Conflicts

An IAC exists whenever there is a resort to armed force between states.[13] IHL applies from that moment. There is no requirement for the armed force to last for an extended period of time or for it to attain a certain level of intensity. In this sense, regardless of how Ukraine and/or Russia have categorized the situation, an IAC began the moment Russia initiated its military intervention in Crimea; from that moment, IHL formally applied to Russia and Ukraine. For IHL to apply, neither a declaration of war nor an acknowledgement by the parties to the armed conflict that an armed conflict exists is required. The factual circumstances determine whether IHL applies.[14] In addition, IHL applies to all cases of a declared war between states, even if there is no resort to armed force.[15]

---

12　See, e.g., the Letter dated 14 September 2016 from the Permanent Representative of Ukraine to the United Nations addressed to the Secretary General, A/71/379–S/2016/788, 15 September 2016; and Council on Foreign Relations, Global Conflict Tracker, Conflict in Ukraine | Global Conflict Tracker (cfr.org) (accessed 30 November 2021).
13　The Prosecutor v. Dusko Tadić, (IT-94-1-A), Decision on the Defence Motion for Interlocutory Appeal on Jurisdiction, 2 October 1995, para. 70.
14　International Committee of the Red Cross (ICRC), Geneva Convention for the Amelioration of the Condition of the Wounded and Sick in Armed Forces in the Field (First Geneva Convention), 12 August 1949, 75 UNTS 31, art 2 and The Prosecutor v. Dusko Tadić, (IT-94-1-A), Decision on the Defence Motion for Interlocutory Appeal on Jurisdiction, 2 October 1995, para. 70.
15　International Committee of the Red Cross (ICRC), Geneva Convention for the Amelioration of the Condition of the Wounded and Sick in Armed Forces in the Field (First Geneva Convention), 12 August 1949, 75 UNTS 31, art. 2.

Conflicts between states and non-state armed groups are discussed in more detail below. However, there are certain situations where these types of conflict are classified as IACs and not as NIACs. When a state has a certain amount of control over an organized armed group, the conflict is classified as an IAC instead of an NIAC. The International Criminal Tribunal for the former Yugoslavia (ICTY) established that partial state control or influence is not enough to lead to change the classification of an armed conflict; the respective state must have "overall control" over the organized armed group.[16] According to the ICTY, a state has overall control when it "has a role in organizing, co-ordinating or planning the military actions of the military group, in addition to financing, training and equipping or providing operational support to that group".[17] The involvement of the state must therefore go beyond mere logistical support or aid; however, the state does not have to be involved in every action that the group takes.

IHL applies in relation to IACs until a general peaceful conclusion is reached between the belligerent states, usually in the form of some type of peace agreement. During an ongoing IAC, IHL applies throughout the whole territory (including the territorial waters and airspace) of the belligerent parties, even if there are no active hostilities in an area. In addition, IHL applies on the high seas, or in international waters beyond states' internal or territorial waters.[18] Certain

---

16  International courts such as the ICTY constitute recognized sources of international law according to article 38 of the ICJ Statute. This means that the formulations about a case processed by the ICTY can be used as future references regarding how a specific aspect, in this case the classification of armed conflict, is to be interpreted.
17  Prosecutor v. Dusko Tadic (Appeal Judgement), IT-94-1-A, International Criminal Tribunal for the former Yugoslavia (ICTY), 15 July 1999, para 137.
18  The Prosecutor v. Dusko Tadić, (IT-94-1-A), Decision on the Defence Motion for Interlocutory Appeal on Jurisdiction, 2 October 1995, para. 70.

rules continue to apply even after the end of an IAC, such as those relating to individuals who have been deprived of their liberty and who are protected until they have been released.[19]

## The Law of Belligerent Occupation

A belligerent occupation is a special form of IAC case that triggers a subset of rules specifically designed to regulate situations in which one state takes control of another state's territory without permission. The general IHL idea underlying the legal regulation of belligerent occupation is that such an occupation is temporary, lasting only until the *status quo ante* is reinstated.[20] As a matter of international law, occupied territory cannot be annexed by the occupying state. Furthermore, in line with the principle of "no fruit of aggression", no state shall recognize the acquisition of territory resulting from an act of aggression.[21] Similarly, the assumed allegiance of the civilian population in the occupied territory does not change.

Belligerent occupations are often the result of an invasion that coincides with fighting between two states. However, belligerent occupations also include situations where a state takes control of part of another state without armed resistance. As long as such control is non-consensual, the law of belligerent occupation applies. This may also result from the withdrawal of consent to the presence of foreign armed forces on the territory of a state.

---

19  International Committee of the Red Cross (ICRC), Additional Protocol to the Geneva Conventions of 12 August 1949, and relating to the Protection of Victims of International Armed Conflicts (Protocol I), 8 June 1977, 1125 UNTS 3, 3(b).
20  UN General Assembly, Definition of Aggression, A/RES/3314, art 5(3), 14 December 1974.
21  United Nations, General Assembly, Definition of Aggression, 14 December 1974, A/RES/3314, art 5(3).

The mere fact that a foreign state's troops are present on another state's territory is not sufficient for the territory to be considered occupied. According to the law of belligerent occupation, a territory is only occupied when it is actually placed under the effective control of a hostile army.[22] Effective control has traditionally been characterized by two features: the physical presence of the occupying power and the ability of the occupying power to exercise authority over the territory concerned. Areas in which hostilities between the parties to an armed conflict are taking place, areas under unclear control, and areas close to being but not under the effective control of the occupying power are not considered occupied.

The belligerent parties' opinions concerning whether or not an area is occupied do not affect the legal status of a territory. It is the factual circumstances that dictate whether an area is occupied or not. By the same token, a belligerent occupation ends in principle when the factual circumstances cease to exist, that is, when a state ceases to exercise effective control over another state's territory in accordance with the criteria presented above. However, some controversy surrounds the question of whether a belligerent occupation can continue, as a matter of law, if and when an occupying power opts not to exercise its effective control despite its ability to do so.[23]

---

22 Convention (IV) respecting the Laws and Customs of War on Land and its annex, Regulations concerning the Laws and Customs of War on Land. The Hague, 18 October 1907, art. 42.
23 On this topic, see, e.g., Y. Dinstein, *The International Law of Belligerent Occupation* (Cambridge: Cambridge University Press, 2009), 44.

## Non-international Armed Conflicts

In contrast to IACs, IHL's application to NIACs depends on two important factors. The conflict has to reach a certain level of intensity and the non-state actor, or actors, must have a certain degree of organization.[24] Other violent situations that do not display these two requirements, such as internal disturbances and tensions, riots and isolated or sporadic acts of violence, fall below the threshold for the application of IHL.[25]

The threshold for the intensity criterion is not specified in any treaty but guidance can be found in jurisprudence, in particular from the decisions of the ICTY. The ICTY has specified multiple factors that are indicative of the requisite level of intensity, such as:

- the number, duration and intensity of confrontations;
- the type of weapons and other military equipment used;
- the number and caliber of munitions fired;
- the number of persons and types of forces participating in the fighting;
- the number of casualties;
- the extent of material destruction;
- the number of civilians fleeing combat zones;
- the involvement of the UN Security Council.[26]

Similarly, the ICTY has identified factors that indicate when an armed group has met the threshold of organization:

- the group has a command structure;
- the group can carry out operations in an organized manner;

---

24 The Prosecutor v. Dusko Tadić, (IT-94-1-A), Decision on the Defence Motion for Interlocutory Appeal on Jurisdiction, 2 October 1995, para. 70.
25 See, e.g., International Committee of the Red Cross (ICRC), Protocol Additional to the Geneva Conventions of 12 August 1949, and relating to the Protection of Victims of Non-International Armed Conflicts (Protocol II), 8 June 1977, 1125 UNTS 609, art 1.
26 The Prosecutor v. Ramush Haradinaj, Idriz Balaj and Lahi Brahimaj, (IT-04-84-T), Judgment, 3 April 2008, para 49.

- the group has a certain level of logistics;
- the group has a level of discipline and the ability to implement the basic obligations of Common Article 3;
- the armed group speaks with one voice.[27]

Thus, an organized armed group does not need to have the same level of organization as the armed forces of a state, but must be organized to a given degree. The armed forces of states are generally presumed to fulfil the organization criterion, but it is possible to imagine situations where the armed forces of a failing state would disintegrate and eventually fall below the threshold of the organization criterion.[28]

Importantly, the IHL applicable to NIACs binds states and organized armed groups alike, and applies from the point that both threshold criteria are met until a peaceful settlement is reached;[29] or, in other words, until the conflict no longer meets the classification of a non-international armed conflict. As noted above, persons deprived of their liberty remain protected by IHL for as long as they remain in that state, even if that situation extends beyond the end of the armed conflict. In addition, the IHL of NIACs applies throughout the territory of a state that is a party to the armed conflict as well as to the territory controlled by an organized armed group that is a party to the armed conflict.

---

[27] The Prosecutor v. Ljube Boškoski and Johan Tarčulovski, (IT-04-82-T), Judgment, 10 July 2008, paras 199-203.

[28] See, e.g., J. K. Kleffner, "The legal fog of an illusion: three reflections on 'organization' and 'intensity' as criteria for the temporal scope of the law of non-international armed conflict", *International Law Studies*, vol. 95, no. 1 (2019): 170-172.

[29] The Prosecutor v. Dusko Tadić, (IT-94-1-A), Decision on the Defence Motion for Interlocutory Appeal on Jurisdiction, 2 October 1995, para. 70.

## The Difference Between the Law on War and the Law on Waging War

International law distinguishes between the law that regulates when states can legitimately use force and IHL, which regulates the conduct during an armed conflict. The laws regulating when states can use force against other states is called *jus ad bellum*. It is regulated chiefly by the UN Charter's prohibition of the use of force against other states and the two exceptions to that prohibition: self-defense and authorization by the UN Security Council.[30] It should be noted, especially in relation to Russia's "passportization"[31] strategy, that self-defense as stipulated in the UN Charter should not be interpreted as allowing the use of force to protect nationals abroad. International law does not provide a regulation of when recourse to force may be lawful in relation to non-state actors, although there is a right to use force to maintain order and security within a state and to suppress insurrections, which stems from the principle of sovereignty.

IHL and *jus ad bellum* exist independently of, and separate from, one another. This means that acts that are unlawful under *jus ad bellum* may still be lawful under IHL and vice versa. For example, a state can act in lawful self-defense but still violate IHL; or a state could be an unlawful aggressor while still adhering to IHL. This separation also means that IHL applies equally to all parties to an armed conflict regardless of the lawfulness or unlawfulness of the use of force under *jus ad bellum*.

---

30 United Nations, Charter of the United Nations, 24 October 1945, 1 UNTS XVI, art 2(4), 42 and 51.
31 Passportization is the mass distribution of Russian citizenship to individuals living outside of Russia.

## Human Rights

In addition to IHL, International Human Rights Law continues to apply during both IACs and NIACs, even though human rights are primarily focused on regulating the relationship between a state and the individuals under its jurisdiction in peacetime.[32] In this case, jurisdiction should be understood as applying as though the individual were on the state's territory, or in a territory over which the state has effective control, or as though the state had effective control over an individual, for example, in a situation where an individual is being detained.

There is some room for the derogation of human rights in times of armed conflict, but no derogation is allowed of certain fundamental human rights such as the right to life, protection against inhumane treatment and torture, the prohibition on slavery and the prohibition against being punished for an act that was not criminalized when committed.[33] Limitations on other human rights must be proportionate and necessary in a democratic society, and are only permissible in pursuit of legitimate interests such as national security or public safety.[34]

Human rights regulate the relationship between the state and individuals. Whether and to what extent organized armed groups have any human rights obligations is controversial. Arguments have been made that under certain circumstances, such as when they take over state functions in a

---

32 C. Greenwood, "Historical development and legal basis", in *The Handbook of International Humanitarian Law*, 2nd edn, edited by Dieter Fleck (New York: Oxford University Press, 2008): 1-44, 12.
33 Council of Europe, European Convention for the Protection of Human Rights and Fundamental Freedoms, as amended by Protocols No. 11 and 14, 4 November 1950, ETS 5.
34 See, e.g., Council of Europe, European Convention for the Protection of Human Rights and Fundamental Freedoms, as amended by Protocols Nos. 11 and 14, 4 November 1950, ETS 5, art 6, 8-11.

territory which they control, organized armed groups assume limited obligations under International Human Rights Law.[35]

## Possible Avenues for Accountability for Violations of International Law

There are a number of possible avenues for holding states and individuals accountable for violations of international law, some of which are also available in cases of violations of IHL and International Human Rights Law in conflict situations. Some of these avenues are discussed below in relation to the conflicts in Ukraine.

### The United Nations Security Council

The UN Charter states that the UN Security Council has primary responsibility for international peace and security.[36] Whenever a threat to international peace and security arises, the Security Council is mandated to take appropriate action to re-establish international peace and security. The Security Council's actions in response to situations that it deems to be threats to international peace and security have ranged from military intervention to peace operations, economic or military sanctions and the establishment of international criminal tribunals.

However, the Security Council is a political body and its binding resolutions are subject to veto by one or more of its five permanent members. The power of veto creates obvious challenges where one of the five veto powers has a political

---

35  See, e.g., A. Clapham, "Human rights obligations of non-state actors in conflict situations", *International Review of the Red Cross*, vol. 88, no. 863 (September 2006): 491-523; and Y. Ronen, "Human rights obligations of territorial non-state actors", *Cornell International Law Journal*, vol. 46, no. 1 (2013): 21.
36  Charter of the United Nations, 24 October 1945, 1 UNTS XVI, art 24(1).

interest that is not in line with the will of the rest of the Council.

### International Courts and Judicial Proceedings

A second possible avenue for accountability can be found in international courts and judicial proceedings. There have been, and continue to be, a number of international processes relating to the situation in Ukraine. Ukraine has made multiple interstate applications to the European Court of Human Rights in relation to alleged human rights violations by Russia (nine as of September 2021), and Russia has made one such interstate application in relation to Ukraine.[37]

By virtue of a so-called "12(3) declaration", Ukraine has given the International Criminal Court (ICC) jurisdiction over potential war crimes and crimes against humanity within its borders since February 20, 2014.[38] According to this declaration, even though Ukraine is not a party to the Court, the ICC's jurisdiction covers any actions taken on the territory of Ukraine, including any Russian violations in eastern Ukraine or Crimea.[39]

Ukraine has also filed claims against Russia, and requested provisional measures of protection, at the International Court of Justice (ICJ).[40] These claims relate to possible Russian financing of terrorism in violation of the International Convention for the Suppression of the Financing of

---

[37] ECHR, Inter-state applications by date of introduction of the applications, 23 July 2021, https://www.echr.coe.int/Documents/InterState_applications_ENG.pdf
[38] There was an earlier declaration made by Ukraine but with a much more limited scope, see https://www.icc-cpi.int/ukraine
[39] Office of the Prosecutor, "ICC Prosecutor extends preliminary examination of the situation in Ukraine following second article 12(3) declaration", 29 September 2015, https://www.icc-cpi.int/Pages/item.aspx?name=pr1156
[40] ICJ, Application of the International Convention for the Suppression of the Financing of Terrorism and of the International Convention on the Elimination of All Forms of Racial Discrimination (Ukraine v. Russian Federation), https://www.icj-cij.org/en/case/166

Terrorism,[41] and possible Russian racial discrimination, violating the International Convention on the Elimination of All Forms of Racial Discrimination.[42] The ICJ has found that it has jurisdiction in both instances and, as of autumn 2021, is moving forward with them.[43]

Interstate arbitration between Ukraine and Russia is also ongoing at the Permanent Court of Arbitration relating to navigational rights, marine resources and the marine environment in the Black Sea and the Sea of Azov (the sea between Crimea and Russia);[44] an Award on Preliminary Objections was issued in February 2020.[45] Further, there have been arbitral proceedings linked to the International Tribunal for the Law of the Sea concerning the detention of three Ukrainian naval vessels and 24 Ukrainian seamen.[46] In this case, the

---

41 UN General Assembly, International Convention for the Suppression of the Financing of Terrorism, 9 December 1999, no. 38349.
42 United Nations, General Assembly, International Convention on the Elimination of All Forms of Racial Discrimination, 21 December 1965, United Nations, Treaty Series, vol. 660, 195.
43 Application of the International Convention for the Suppression of the Financing of Terrorism and of the International Convention on the Elimination of All Forms of Racial Discrimination (Ukraine v. Russian Federation), Preliminary Objections, Judgment, 8 November 2019, para. 134.
44 In the matter of a dispute concerning costal state rights in the Black Sea, Sea of Azov and Kerch Strait before an arbitral tribunal constituted under ANNEX VII to the 1982 United Nations Convention on the Law of the Sea between Ukraine and the Russian Federation, the Permanent Court of Arbitration, Written observations and submissions of Ukraine on jurisdiction, PCA Case No. 2017-06, 27 November 2018, para 9-10.
45 Dispute Concerning Coastal State Rights in the Black Sea, Sea of Azov, and Kerch Strait (Ukraine v. the Russian Federation), Permanent Court of Arbitration, https://pca-cpa.org/en/cases/149/
46 Case concerning the detention of three Ukrainian naval vessels (Ukraine v. Russian Federation), Provisional Measures, International Tribunal for the Law of the Sea, https://www.itlos.org/en/main/cases/list-of-cases/case-concerning-the-detention-of-three-ukrainian-naval-vessels-ukraine-v-russian-federation-provisional-measures/

Tribunal ordered the release of the vessels and seamen on May 25, 2019.[47]

In addition to interstate proceedings, a number of individuals have made applications to the European Court of Human Rights. As of July 2021, there had been over 7,000 individual applications in relation to the situation in eastern Ukraine and Crimea since 2014.[48]

**National Courts**

Another possible avenue for accountability for violations of International Law, and of IHL in particular, would be national courts—whether Ukrainian, Russian or those of third states. This avenue is possible given that national courts have jurisdiction over alleged violations, especially when they amount to war crimes or other international crimes, such as crimes against humanity, and possibly in some instances the crime of aggression.[49] However, a number of difficulties arise with such national proceedings. For instance, there may be concerns regarding the independence and/or impartiality of domestic court proceedings in the states most directly involved. Furthermore, it has proved to be a long and difficult process to secure evidence, witnesses and suspects in uncooperative states, and in territory controlled by uncooperative entities as with, for instance, Crimea and eastern Ukraine. Thus, only a few domestic proceedings have been initiated, such as the ongoing procedures relating to the downing of

---

47  Case concerning the detention of three Ukrainian naval vessels, Ukraine v Russian Federation, Provisional measures, ITLOS Case No. 26, ICGJ 542 (ITLOS 2019), 25th May 2019.
48  Press country profile Russia, ECHR, updated July 2021, https://www.echr.coe.int/Documents/CP_Russia_ENG.pdf, 32
49  See, e.g., the Swedish law Lag (2014: 406) om straff för folkmord, brott mot mänskligheten och krigsförbrytelser and Regeringens proposition 2020/21:204, Aggressionsbrottet I svensk rätt och svensk straffrättslig domsrätt.

flight MH17 on July 17, 2014 in Donets'kaia Oblast, Ukraine;[50] and some national proceedings based on international agreements,[51] such as the case of Aeroport Belbek LLC and Igor Valerievich Kolomoisky vs the Russian Federation.[52]

Moreover, a trend can be observed in relation to alleged cybercrime, hacking and espionage where, for instance, the United States has indicted the citizens of another state for allegedly acting on behalf of that state. These cases may be pursued not to achieve a swift trial, at least not principally, but to send a message about possible accountability and demonstrate that legal attributions can be made.[53] Pursuing accountability by indicting individuals may become a future avenue in cases beyond the issue of cyberspace, such as issues involving proxy actors or covert operations.

## Challenges

As demonstrated above, while some international procedures deal specifically with violations of IHL, many ongoing judicial processes are related to other areas of international law. Some of the international courts that have prosecuted war crimes, such as the ICTY and the International Criminal Tribunal for Rwanda, were established by United Nations

---

50  For more information, see https://www.courtmh17.com/en/about-the-case.html
51  Examples include the Agreement between the Government of the Russian Federation and the Cabinet of the Ministers of Ukraine on the Encouragement and Mutual Protection of Investments, 27 November 1998, https://www.italaw.com/sites/default/files/laws/italaw11854.pdf
52  Aeroport Belbek LLC and Igor Valerievich Kolomoisky v. The Russian Federation, Permanent Court of Arbitration (PCA), https://pca-cpa.org/en/cases/123/
53  See, e.g., United States of America v. Borisovich Netyksho, Alekseyevich Antonov, Sergeyevich Badin, Sergeyevich Yermakov, Viktorovich Lukashev, Aleksandrovich Morgachev, Yurevich Kozachek, Vyacheslavovich Yeshov, Andreyevich Malyshev, Vladimirovich Osadchuk, Aleksandrovich Potemkin and Sergeyevich Kovalev, Indictment, Case 1:18-cr-00215-ABJ, 13 July 2018 (The United States District Court for the District of Columbia I). Cases have also been initiated against North Korean and Chinese citizens.

Security Council resolutions. This would in all likelihood not be feasible with regard to the conflict areas of Eastern Europe, as Russia would almost certainly veto any such resolution. Moreover, the ICC was established to make it unnecessary to create ad hoc international courts. However, international recognition of or accession to the ICC has been relatively limited. In relation to the conflicts in Eastern Europe, Armenia, Azerbaijan, Russia and Ukraine have all failed to ratify the Rome Statute. States could, however, make a 12(3) declaration, as Ukraine has done, to give the ICC temporary jurisdiction.

In addition, many of the international courts and tribunals, including the ICC and the European Court of Human Rights, are based on the idea that cases are only admissible if and when national court proceedings have been exhausted and/or proved inadequate. In the case of the ICC, this means that it only handles cases that national courts cannot or will not adjudicate in a free and fair manner. In relation to individual plaintiffs at the European Court of Human Rights, the respective state's domestic remedies must have been exhausted, or have proved unavailable or ineffective.

Furthermore, in contrast to national courts, international courts lack the support of an executive branch, which means that the courts need the support of state parties whenever there is a potential case, or an indicted individual. This can create difficult situations when potential violations are state-orchestrated or state-supported, and makes it difficult for international courts to get access to the relevant evidence, witnesses and suspects. This issue is further complicated by the fact that many of the potential violations take place far away from the courts, often in areas that are not—or not fully—controlled by a state.

Jurisdiction is an issue that has been discussed in relation to many procedures.[54] In some instances, in order to be able to decide which law is applicable, the courts have had to determine which state has had effective control over or jurisdiction in a certain area at a certain time. International courts have been cautious about dealing with this in relation to the conflict situation in Ukraine.[55] For instance, for the European Court of Human Rights to determine whether Russia has committed human rights violations in the non-government-controlled parts of eastern Ukraine, it would have to determine whether Russia had effective control over or extraterritorial jurisdiction in those areas, which in turn might be indicative of whether the areas were occupied at the time. In these and other highly politically sensitive cases, international courts can display a certain degree of reluctance to engage, employing a number of avoidance doctrines. In the case of proceedings before the European Court of Human Rights, for instance, an ever-evolving jurisprudence regarding what it takes for a state to exercise its "jurisdiction", and the ensuing obligations under the European Convention, is illustrative.

## Concluding Thoughts

While it may seem that little is happening on the legal front in relation to potential violations of International Law in Eastern Europe, the above examples show how, where and when

---

54  See, e.g., M. Milanovic, "ECtHR Grand Chamber declares admissible the case of Ukraine v. Russia re Crimea", EJIL: Talk!, 15 January 2021, https://www.ejiltalk.org/ecthr-grand-chamber-declares-admissible-the-case-of-ukraine-v-russia-re-crimea/; and G. Nuridzhanian, "Ukraine vs. Russia in International Courts and Tribunals", EJIL: Talk!, 9 March 2016, https://www.ejiltalk.org/ukraine-versus-russia-in-international-courts-and-tribunals/.
55  They have, however, made statements in relation to other situations, such as Russian control over parts of Georgia.

International Humanitarian Law is applicable in relation to potential violations, and that there are avenues for accountability in relation to various violations of International Law. The process of accountability in the international community takes time and there are many obstacles that must be overcome. Nonetheless, the process of accountability is ongoing and while the results of adjudications might not be the desired ones, most processes will in time reach a conclusion.

*Dr. Marika Ericson is Head of, and Isak Malm is a Research Assistant at, the Centre for International and Operational Law of the Swedish Defence University in Stockholm.*